GREAT SCIENTISTS

Geneticists

Cavendish Square
New York

Published in 2014 by Cavendish Square Publishing, LLC
303 Park Avenue South, Suite 1247, New York, NY 10010

First Edition

Website: cavendishsq.com

CPSIA Compliance Information: Batch #WW14CSQ

All websites were available and accurate when this book was sent to press.

Library of Congress Cataloging-in-Publication Data
Laubichler, Manfred D.
Geneticists / by Manfred D. Laubichler, et. al.
p. cm. — (Great scientists)
Includes index.
ISBN 978-1-62712-551-2 (hardcover) ISBN 978-1-62712-552-9 (paperback) ISBN 978-1-62712-553-6 (ebook)
1. Geneticists — Biography — Juvenile literature. I. Laubichler, Manfred Dietrich. II. Title.
QH437.5 2014
~~575.1~~ d23

Editorial Director: Dean Miller; Editorial Assistant: Amy Hayes; Art Director: Jeffrey Talbot; Designer: Joseph Macri; Production Manager: Jennifer Ryder-Talbot; Production Editor: Andrew Coddington; Photo Researchers: Laurie Platt Winfrey, Carousel Research, Inc.; Joseph Marci; Amy Greenan; and Julie Alissi, J8 Media

The photographs in this book are used by permission and through the courtesy of: Front cover photos by SSPL/Hulton Archive/Getty Images, Everett Collection/SuperStock, SCIENCE SOURCE/Photo Researchers/Getty Images, AP Photo/Salk Institute, HO; Back cover photo by © Jewish Chronicle, AP Photo/Alastair Grant, courtesy California Institute of Technology; SSPL/Hulton Archive/Getty Images, 1; Everett Collection/SuperStock, 6; SCIENCE SOURCE/Photo Researchers/Getty Images, 6; AP Photo/Salk Institute, HO, 6; © Jewish Chronicle, 7; AP Photo/Alastair Grant, 7; courtesy California Institute of Technology, 7; DIBYANGSHU SARKAR/Stringer/AFP/Getty Images, 8; UniversalImagesGroup/Contributor/Universal Images Group/Getty Images, 12; Accurate Art, Inc., 13, 19, 25, 79, 86, 90, 95, 98, 102; © AP Images, 15; AP Photo/Paul Sakuma, 17; AP Photo/Paul Sakuma, 21; DANIEL MORDZINSKI/Staff/AFP/Getty Images, 24; AP Photo/de la Mauviniere, 28; AP Photo/Paul Sakuma, 31; NLM/Science Source/Photo Researchers/Getty Images, 34; Hulton Archive/Stringer/Hulton Archive/Getty Images, 36; WalterGilbert2/ nlm.nih.gov, 40; ©AP Images, 42; Hans Wild/Contributor/Time & Life Pictures/Getty Images, 45; © iStockphoto.com/4x6, 48; Dpryan/Rhodopson-transducin, 51; DEA PICTURE LIBRARY/Contributor/De Agostini/Getty Images, 53; Janet Stephens/Wistar rat/visualsonline.cancer.gov/details.cfm?imageid=2568, 56; Steve Northup/Contributor/TIME & LIFE Images/Getty Images, 59; Hulton Archive/Stringer/Hulton Archive/Getty Images, 62; AP Photo/Josh Reynolds, File, 65; Joshua Lederberg lab/ profiles.nlm.nih.gov/BB/B/A/A/W/_/bbbaaw_.jpg, 68; SCIENCE SOURCE/Photo Researchers/Getty Images, 71; AP Photo/Michael Probst, 75; Gavrilov S.A./ Koltushi Mendel'/Own work/Creative Commons CC0 1.0 Universal Public Domain Dedication, Keystone-France/Contributor/Gamma-Keystone/Getty Images, 81; SCIENCE SOURCE/Photo Researchers/Getty Images, 85; Herbert Gehr/Contributor/Time & Life Pictures/Getty Images, 89; MacVicar, N. — National Institutes of Health/Marshall Nirenberg performing experiment/profiles.nlm.nih.gov/JJ/B/B/D/F/_/jjbbdf_.jpg, 93; Pbroks13/Punnett Square/Own work/Creative Commons Attribution-Share Alike 3.0 Unported license/GNU Free Documentation License, 97; Keystone/Staff/Hulton Archive/Getty Images, 100; Keystone/Stringer/Hulton Archive/Getty Images, 105; Bryn Mawr College Staff Photographer/Nettie Stevens microscope (2)/Courtesy of Bryn Mawr College Special Collections/Creative Commons Attribution 3.0 Unported license, 109; © iStockphoto.com/Antagain, 111; AP Photo/Stephan Savoia, 113; Therese Schwartze/Hugo de Vries (1848-1935), by Thérèse Schwartze (1851-1918)/ Universiteitsmuseum Amsterdam, 116; Cold Spring Harbor Laboratory/James D Watson Genome Image/National Human Genome Research Institute, 118; AP Photo/F. Carter Smith, 122; AP Photo/Bob Child, 124; AP Photo/Alastair Grant, 127; AP Photo/Paul Clements, 130.

Printed in the United States of America

An Introduction to Great Scientists: *Geneticists*

GREAT SCIEN TISTS

Science offers an ever-expanding and seemingly ever-changing array of facts and theories to explain the workings of life and the universe. Behind its doors, we can explore fascinating worlds ranging from the tiny—the spiral ladder of DNA in every human cell and the particle zoo of quarks and mesons in every atom—to the unimaginably vast—the gradual, often catastrophic shifting of continents over the globe and the immense gravitational fields surrounding black holes in space. Unfortunately, the doors of science often remain shut to students and the general public, who worry they are unable to understand the work done in these technical fields.

Great Scientists seeks to serve as a key. Its goal is to introduce many notable researchers and concepts, sparking interest and providing jumping-off points for gaining further knowledge. To this end, these books offer a select survey of scientists and their accomplishments across disciplines, throughout history, and around the world. The life stories of these individuals and the descriptions of their research and advancements will prove informational and inspirational to budding scientists and to all those with inquisitive minds. For some, learning the paths of these scientists' lives will enable ambitious young students to follow in their footsteps.

Science disciplines are foundational by nature. The work done by the earliest pioneers in a specific field often leads to inspire and inform the next generation of minds, who take the findings and discoveries of their heroes and mentors and further the body of knowledge in a certain area. This progress of scientific inquiry and discovery increases the world's understanding of existing theories and tenants, blazing trails into new directions of study. Perhaps by reading this work, the next great geneticists will discover their spark of creativity. Whether interested in the theoretical sciences, mathematics, or the applied fields of engineering and invention, students will find these life stories proof that individuals from any background can be responsible for key discoveries and paradigm-shifting thoughts and experiments.

The Organization of *Geneticists*

This volume profiles more than three dozen representative figures in the history of genetics. Entries are usually 800 to 1,700 words in length, with some longer essays covering individuals who made numerous significant contributions to the development of their fields, such as Gregor Mendel, James Watson, Francis Crick, Rosalind Franklin, Frederick Sanger, Barbara McClintock, and Thomas Morgan. In addition to celebrating famous names that made great strides in scientific inquiry and paved the way for others to follow, the book gives credit to individuals and groups who have gone largely unrecognized, such as women and minorities, as well as many contemporary scientists and researchers who are making the newest advances.

The profile of each scientist begins with a list of the scientist's areas of achievement, as many of these individuals had impact in more than one discipline. Jacques Lucien Monod made significant contributions in the fields of bacteriology and medicine, as well as genetics. Many more like him had such an influence in multiple sciences that inclusion in several different books would be logical, but choices were made to place each scientist in the field most emblematic of his or her work. After a brief statement of that individual's contribution to science, a timeline covers major life events, including birth and death dates, major awards and honors, and milestones in the scientist's education, research, employment, and private life. The entry then details the struggles and triumphs that characterize the lives of many who pursue knowledge as a career.

The Science Behind the Scientist

An important goal of the Great Scientist series is to expand the reader's understanding of science, not just cover the biographical data of specific scientists. To that end, each profile contains one or more sidebars within the article that provide a simple snapshot introduction to a key topic within the featured scientist's achievements, including theories, research, inventions, or discoveries.

While the scientific subjects are not covered in painstaking detail, there is enough information for readers to gain a working knowledge of topics important to the fields of genetics.

Illustrating the Science

Several of the sidebars in this book are accompanied by diagrams that help to reinforce the information presented through graphical representation of complex theories and discoveries. In addition, wherever possible, a photograph, painting, or sculpture of the scientist is provided, although there are no likenesses for some of history's earliest contributors.

Additional Resources

Each profile ends with a two-part bibliography, pointing readers to some of the most significant books and papers written by the particular scientist, as well as other content written about the subject and field of study. It's worth noting that these bibliographies are selected works and by no means a complete listing—many of these scientists have contributed dozens of works. The book concludes with a glossary that offers clear definitions of selected terms and concepts, and a comprehensive index that allows readers to locate information about the people, concepts, organizations, and topics covered throughout the book.

Skill Development for Students

Great Scientists: Geneticists can serve as a basic biographical text on a specific individual or as a source of enrichment for students looking to know more about an entire scientific field. It is an excellent reference for reading and writing assignments, and it can be a foundational beginning of major research and term papers. The bibliographies at the end of the profiles and sidebars are invaluable for students looking to learn more and delve deeper yet into these fascinating subjects.

Sidney Altman

Disciplines: Cell biology, chemistry, and genetics

Contribution: An esteemed molecular biologist, Altman won the Nobel Prize in Chemistry for his discovery of the catalytic properties of ribonucleic acid (RNA).

May 7, 1939	Born in Montreal, Canada
1960	Earns a B.S. in physics from the Massachusetts Institute of Technology (MIT)
1967	Earns a Ph.D. in biophysics from the University of Colorado
1969-1971	Works with the Medical Research Counsel in Cambridge, England
1971	Appointed assistant professor of biology at Yale University
1980	Named professor of biology at Yale
1985-1989	Serves as dean of Yale College
1988	Elected a member of the American Academy of Arts and Sciences
1989	Wins the Nobel Prize in Chemistry
1990	Appointed Sterling Professor of Biology at Yale
1990	Elected a member of the National Academy of Sciences
1990	Elected a member of the American Philosophical Society
1990-1995	Serves on the Board of Governors of the Weizmann Institute of Science
1991-1994	Named a Fellow of the Whitney Humanities Center at Yale
1993	Appointed to the UNESCO International Committee on Bioethics

Early Life

Sidney Altman was born in Montreal, Canada, to parents who were recent emigrants from Eastern Europe. He grew up in Montreal's Jewish community, where Albert Einstein was a hero and learning and education were considered to be the highest goals. Through books, Altman discovered his early interest in science. Reading Selig Hecht's *Explaining the Atom* (1947), he was struck by the simplicity and beauty of the periodic table.

Consequently, he enrolled as a physics major at the Massachusetts Institute of Technology (MIT). He also played ice hockey on the MIT team. During his senior year, Altman discovered the charm of laboratory work in physics. While at MIT, he attended Cyrus Levinthal's course on molecular biology, which provided him with an introduction to this emerging field.

Altman graduated with a B.S. in physics and went on to do graduate work in physics at Columbia University but dropped out after one year.

Catalytic RNA and the RNA World

Several ribonucleic acid (RNA) molecules have catalytic properties and can function as enzymes. RNA has both essential properties of a self-replicating system: information storage and enzymatic activities.

The discovery of catalytic properties of RNA by Altman and Thomas R. Cech radically changed two areas of biological knowledge: the long-held assumption that all enzymes are proteins was overturned, and the problem of the origin of life has been seen in a different light.

All life on Earth is based on chemical reactions that take place within cells and organisms. These biochemical reactions are regulated by catalysts called enzymes. The complex biochemical machinery of a cell cannot function without the presence of specific enzymes for every single reaction. Up to the early 1980s, it was accepted scientific knowledge that every enzyme could be identified with a particular protein. Altman showed that this paradigm no longer holds for all catalysts.

In 1983, he and his coworkers identified an RNA molecule that had all the properties of an enzyme—biological origin, catalysis in the chemical sense, and specificity with respect to its reaction—except that it was not a protein. They found that the RNA component of the enzyme RNase P catalyzes a reaction that cuts a precursor transfer RNA (tRNA) molecule at a specific site. At the same time, Cech demonstrated that another RNA molecule could catalyze a reaction that cuts out a specific segment of itself in the absence of any other enzymes. As a consequence, the standard definition of an enzyme had to be changed. Enzymes could no longer be identified with a specific class of molecules (proteins), but had to be defined in strictly functional terms.

The discovery of catalytic properties of RNA also affected theories about the origin of life on Earth. Previously, the first self-replicating systems were considered to have RNA to store information and proteins to provide all the enzymatic activities needed for reproduction. Such systems are already very complex.

With the discovery of catalytic RNA, a simpler system can be envisioned. An initial RNA world consisting of self-replicating RNA molecules would have been the first stage in the evolution of life. These RNA molecules were capable of a variety of complicated reactions. They could remove parts of their sequence—precursors of the introns in the molecular structure of modern genes—and insert them again. This mechanism already allowed for different combinations of sequences to evolve, an equivalent to the effects of sexual recombination.

At the next step, these RNA molecules began to synthesize proteins, and later deoxyribonucleic acid (DNA) replaced RNA as the molecule of choice for information storage. The enzymatic properties of RNA molecules today as well as the peculiar exon/intron structure of modern genes are a residual of the original processes in the RNA world.

Bibliography

Eigen, Manfred and Ruthild Winkler-Oswatitsch. *Steps Towards Life: A Perspective on Evolution.* Oxford, England: Oxford University Press, 1992.

Altman was frustrated with Columbia's emphasis on classroom courses in the early years of graduate studies and depressed by the death of a close friend. He then worked as poetry and science editor for the Collier Publishing Company. His interest in literature and the humanities continued throughout his career.

Return to Academia

A position as science writer at the National Center for Atmospheric Research brought Altman to Boulder, Colorado, in 1963. There, he met George Gamow, who encouraged him to pursue graduate studies in biophysics. This was one of many lucky coincidences in Altman's career; as he explained, "I always met the right people at the right time."

In 1967, he received his Ph.D. and left Boulder for Harvard University and later University of Cambridge, England, where he pursued postdoctoral work with the top scientists in the field of molecular biology—Matthew Meselson, Sydney Brenner, Francis Crick, and Frederick Sanger.

Cambridge and Early Work on RNA

At Cambridge, Altman started a line of work for which he would eventually be awarded the Nobel Prize in Chemistry. Working with John Smith, he found a mutant ribonucleic acid (RNA) transcript that contained the genomic sequence for one of the transfer RNA (tRNA) molecules, tRNA-Try, that was much longer than the regular tRNA molecule. He also found that after treatment with an extract of normal cells of *Escherichia coli*, the longer transcript could be trimmed to its regular length. The identification of immature tRNA and its processing got him an appointment as assistant professor in the department of biology at Yale University in 1971.

The Detection of Catalytic RNA

At Yale, Altman continued his studies on tRNA processing. He was able to identify an enzyme, called RNase P, which is involved in cutting the original transcript. While investigating the question of how this enzyme could cut the initial transcript of tRNA at a specific position, Altman and his coworkers discovered that RNase P has a protein and a RNA component. This was a major discovery, until then no enzyme was known to have a RNA component. Further studies revealed that the catalytic subunit of the enzyme RNase P is the RNA component.

This result was met with considerable skepticism. Conventional biological wisdom held that any enzyme is a protein. Altman's discovery that RNA can function as an enzyme led to the revision of this long-held principle. At the same time, Thomas R. Cech identified a large RNA molecule that could cut itself without any protein involved in the process. For their discoveries of the catalytic properties of RNA, Altman and Cech were awarded the Nobel Prize in Chemistry in 1989.

The discovery of the catalytic properties of RNA led to new avenues of biological research. The chicken-and-egg problem of the origin of life—deoxyribonucleic acid (DNA) is necessary to make proteins, and proteins are necessary to copy DNA—no longer seemed to be inevitable. A world of RNA molecules is now considered to be the first stage in the evolution of life on Earth. In addition, on the medical front, promising developments inhibiting the replication of human immunodeficiency virus (HIV) resulted from the application of RNA enzymes.

Dean of Yale College

From 1985 until 1989, Altman served as dean of Yale College. Under his leadership, the faculty revised the core curriculum to strengthen the science requirements. He also established a tutorial program in science and mathematics. In the 1990s, he was elected to several prestigious organizations and served on many committees.

Bibliography

By Altman

"Aspects of Biochemical Catalysis," *Cell*, 1984.

"Ribonuclease P: An Enzyme with a Catalytic RNA Subunit," *Advances in Enzymology and Related Areas of Molecular Biology*, 1989.

"Enzymatic Cleavage of RNA by RNA," *Angewandte Chemie*, 1990.

"RNA Enzyme-Directed Gene Therapy," *Proceedings of the National Academy of Sciences*, 1993.

"RNase P in Research and Therapy" *Biotechnology*, 1995.

About Altman

James Laylin K., ed. *Nobel Laureates in Chemistry, 1901-1992*. Washington, D.C.: American Chemical Society, 1993.

Magill, Frank N., ed. "Sidney Altman." in *The Nobel Prize Winners: Chemistry*. Pasadena, Calif.: Salem Press, 1990.

(Manfred D. Laubichler)

William Bateson

Disciplines: Genetics and zoology

Contribution: Bateson introduced Gregor Mendel's work to Great Britain. His breeding experiments established basic Mendelian phenomena for plants and animals.

Aug. 8,1861	Born in Yorkshire, England
1883	Receives a B.A. from University of Cambridge
1885	Elected a Fellow of St. John's College, University of Cambridge
1894	Publishes *Materials for the Study of Variation*
1894	Elected a Fellow of the Royal Society of London
1900	Reads Gregor Mendel's paper on crossing pea plants
1902	Publishes *Mendel's Principles of Heredity: A Defence*
1904	Awarded the Darwin Medal of the Royal Society
1904-1910	Conducts research with E. R. Saunders and Reginald Crundall Punnett
1908-1910	Serves as a professor of biology at University of Cambridge
1909	Publishes Mendel's *Principles of Heredity*
1910	Becomes director of the John Innes Horticultural Institution, London
1910	Founds the *Journal of Genetics* with Punnett
Feb. 8, 1926	Dies in Merton, London, England

Early Life

William Bateson was born on August 8, 1861. His father, William Henry Bateson, was Master of St John's College, Cambridge. He was educated at Rugby and St. John's College, University of Cambridge where he earned first-class honors in the natural science tripos (honors examination). Excelling in embryology and zoology, he received a B.A. in 1883. During several research trips to the United States, Bateson studied marine biology and met W. H. Brooks at The Johns Hopkins University. In 1885, he became a Fellow of St. John's College.

Journeys to central Asia and Egypt sharpened his observational skills and also his interest in evolutionary theory, particularly the origin of species. Returning to University of Cambridge, Bateson focused on the nature of variation as the key to evolutionary change. By surveying the existing literature and making direct observations, Bateson amassed many examples of variation in plants and animals.

Mutations and Mendelism

Upon examining the evidence, Bateson determined that saltations, or discontinuous variations, drove evolutionary change. Attacking natural selection's focus on continuity, *Bateson's Materials for the Study of Variation Treated with Especial Regard to Discontinuity in the Origin of Species* (1894) rejected the idea that adaptive agents alone directed evolution. Saltations, he argued, arose from forces internal to the organism and new characters persisted regardless of adaptive value. He concluded that "the discontinuity of species results from the discontinuity of variation."

Bateson's emphasis on discontinuity led him to appreciate the mutation theory of Dutch botanist Hugo de Vries. De Vries' writings also led Bateson to read the 1865 paper on pea hybridization by Gregor Mendel. Between 1900 and 1902, Bateson became gradually convinced of the universal validity of Mendel's laws.

Controversy with the Biometricians

Opposing natural selection, Bateson drew harsh criticisms from the biometric school led by Walter Weldon and Karl Pearson. Using a statistical approach to continuous variations, the biometricians endorsed natural selection. Personal animosities between Bateson and Weldon added fuel to the fire as Weldon's attacks on Mendel prompted Bateson's response, *Mendel's Principles of Heredity: A Defence* (1902).

However, the controversy reached a turning point at the 1904 meeting of the British Association for the Advancement of Science. As president of the zoological section, Bateson challenged Weldon and he apparently won the ensuing debate with forceful arguments in favor of Mendelism. Gathering supporters to confirm Mendel's laws experimentally, Bateson named the new science "genetics" in 1905.

Complementary Genes

In particular crosses of plants and animals, Bateson and Reginald Crundall Punnett proposed that two different genes act in consort.

A Punnett Square Showing Flower Pigmentation

White CCpp × White ccPP

F_1: Purple CcPp

F_2:

	CP	Cp	pP	cp
CP	CCPP purple	CCPp purple	CcPP purple	CcPp purple
Cp	CCPp purple	CCpp white	CcPp purple	Ccpp white
cP	CcPP purple	CcPp purple	ccPP white	ccPp white
cp	CcPp purple	Ccpp white	ccPp white	ccpp white

When white-flowered sweet pea plants were crossed, the first-generation progeny (F1) all had purple flowers. When these plants were self-fertilized, the second-generation progeny (F2) revealed a ratio of nine purple to seven white. This result can be explained by the presence of two genes for flower pigmentation, P (dominant) or p (recessive) and C or c. Both dominant forms, P and C, must be present in order to produce purple flowers.

One of the early studies of Bateson and Punnett clearly illustrated the notion that two genes can affect a single physical character, or phenotype. Crossing certain strains of white-flowered sweet pea plants resulted in all purple flowers in the first generation (F1) progeny. When these purple-flowered plants self-fertilized, however, the second generation (F2) gave colored flowers in a ratio of nine purple to seven white. In this case, called a dihybrid cross, F2 usually resulted in phenotypic ratios of 9:3:3:1, meaning four kinds of offspring.

Bateson and Punnett's result was unexpected and seemingly inexplicable. To explain the appearance of only two phenotypic classes, they suggested that two different gene pairs contributed to the production of the purple pigment. Purple flowers, therefore, required the presence of both genes. Consequently, the two original white-flowered parents had to be genetically different.

Later researchers confirmed the presence of two dominant genes, designated C and P, needed for the development of purple flowers. The absence of one or both of these complementary genes results in white flowers.

Without contradicting Mendel's laws, Bateson and Punnett's hypothesis convincingly accounted for dihybrid ratios other than the familiar 9:3:3:1. While confirming Mendelian principles, the concept of complementary genes also extended the explanatory scope of Mendelism.

Bibliography

Colin, Edward C. *Elements of Genetics.* New York: McGraw-Hill, 1956.

Gardner, Eldon J. *Principle of Genetics.* 4th ed. New York: John Wiley & Sons, 1972.

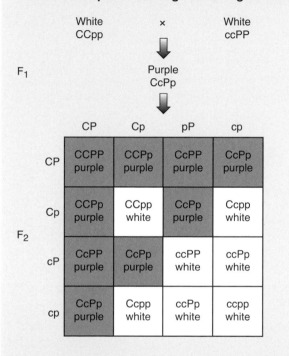

Bateson's Achievement

Bateson's collaboration with L. Doncaster, E. R. Saunders, and Reginald Crundall Punnett confirmed that Mendel's laws applied to animals as well as to plants. Furthermore, breeding experiments with sweet peas and domestic fowl extended Mendelism to phenomena such as reversion, coupling, and complementary factors.

After persistent funding difficulties at University of Cambridge, Bateson left in 1910 to become director of the John Innes Horticultural Institution. The same year, he cofounded the *Journal of Genetics* with Punnett. Although rejecting new ideas in his later years, Bateson is commonly regarded as the founder of the first school of Mendelian genetics.

Bibliography

By Bateson

Materials for the Study of Variation Treated with Especial Regard to Discontinuity in the Origin of Species, 1894.

Mendel's Principles of Heredity: A Defence, 1902.

Mendel's Principles of Heredity, 1909.

Problems of Genetics, 1913.

Punnett, R. C., ed. *Scientific Papers of William Bateson*, 1928.

About Bateson

Coleman, William. "Bateson, William." in *Dictionary of Scientific Biography*, edited by Charles Coulston Gillispie. Vol. 1. New York: Charles Scribner's Sons, 1970.

Darden, Lindley. "William Bateson and the Promise of Mendelism." *Journal of the History of Biology* 10 (1977).

Bateson, Beatrice. *William Bateson, F. R. S. Naturalist.* Cambridge, England: Cambridge University Press, 1928.

(Robinson M. Yost)

George Wells Beadle

Disciplines: Cell biology, chemistry, a nd genetics

Contribution: Beadle, a pioneer in the study of the chemical action of genes within cells, helped to demonstrate that genes control specific chemical reactions.

Oct. 22, 1903	Born in Wahoo, Nebraska
1922-1927	Studies at the University of Nebraska
1927-1931	Works on a Ph.D. in biology at Cornell University
1931	Given a National Research Council Fellowship
1931-1937	Works as a research fellow at the California Institute of Technology (Caltech)
1937	Accepts a position at Stanford University
1946	Returns to Caltech as head of the division of biology
1950	Wins the Lasker Award
1953	Receives the Emil Christian Hansen Prize
1958	Shares the Nobel Prize in Physiology or Medicine with Edward L. Tatum and Joshua Lederberg
1959	Wins the National Award of the American Cancer Society
1960	Receives the Kimber Genetics Award of the National Academy of Science
1961-1968	Serves as president of the University of Chicago
June 9, 1989	Dies in Pomona, California

Early Life

George Wells Beadle was born on October 22, 1903 on a farm in Wahoo, Nebraska. His family took to calling him "Beets," a nickname that remained with him throughout his life. Growing up, Beadle planned to take over his father's farm. A teacher at his local high school, however, persuaded him to attend the University of Nebraska College of Agriculture.

Beadle completed his undergraduate degree at Nebraska and decided to stay for an extra year to earn a master's degree. This year of research convinced Beadle that he wanted to commit himself to science. He decided to continue his work at Cornell University, where he earned his Ph.D. in 1931.

Research at Caltech

After finishing his degree, Beadle went to the California Institute of Technology (Caltech) on a National Research Council Fellowship. He began to work on the genetics of the fruit fly *Drosophila melanogaster*. In collaboration with Boris Ephrussi, Beadle made an important discovery about how genes in the flies' cells control the production of the chemical for brown-eye pigment. Based on this research, he became convinced that the study of genetics needed to be approached through chemistry.

Scientific Breakthrough at Stanford

In 1937, Beadle left Caltech to become a professor of biology at Stanford University. He began a collaboration with a biochemist, Edward L. Tatum, to continue to explore the relationship between genes and cell chemistry. Working with a variety of bread mold called *Neurospora*, Beadle and Tatum proved that genes control specific chemical reactions. By doing so, they created a whole new area of research: biochemical genetics, or the study of gene action. Their discovery also helped to explain the similarity between parents and their offspring, since it demonstrated that their similar genes mean that children will be similar to their parents at the level of biochemistry.

From Scientist to Administrator

In 1946, Beadle was lured back to Caltech to become the head of the division of biology. This position made him the leader of one of the most prestigious biology programs in the country. Beadle focused on making Caltech the premier research institution in molecular biology, while maintaining its strength in other areas of biology. His success in this venture brought him renown for his leadership ability.

Beadle's winning of the Nobel Prize in Physiology or Medicine in 1958 for his work while at Stanford confirmed his excellence as a scientist. This affirmation of skills made him an attractive choice to become president of one of the premier research universities in the world, the University of Chicago, in 1961. He served in this capacity until his retirement in 1968.

Back to Maize Research

After retiring as president of the University of Chicago, Beadle remained there as a researcher. He returned to his first research field, the genetics of maize (Indian corn). He continued to be an active researcher well into his seventies. At the end of his life, he returned to Southern California, where he died on June 9, 1989.

Bibliography

By Beadle

An Introduction to Genetics, 1939 (with A. H. Sturtevant).

"Genetic Control of Biochemical Reactions in *Neurospora*," *Proceedings of the National Academy of Sciences*, 1941 (with Edward L. Tatum).

Genetics and Modern Biology, 1963.

The Language of Life: An Introduction to the Science of Genetics, 1966 (with Muriel B. Beadle).

About Beadle

Judson, Horace Freeland. *The Eighth Day of Creation: Makers of the Revolution in Biology*. New York: Simon & Schuster, 1979.

Kay, Lily. *The Molecular Vision of Life: Caltech, the Rockefeller Foundation, and the Rise of the New Biology*. New York: Oxford University Press, 1993.

Olby, Robert. *The Path to the Double Helix*. London: Macmillan, 1974.

(David A. Valone)

One Gene, One Enzyme

The genetic material within cells is used to produce enzymes. Each gene, or region of the genetic material that produces enzymes, produces a single enzyme.

Beadle helped to develop the understanding of how genes function within cells. Prior to his work, scientists had a general understanding that the genetic material of cells was carried on the chromosomes in the cell nucleus, and that some regions of these chromosomes were significant sites controlling the expression of certain inherited characteristics. Scientists still did not know exactly how these important regions of the chromosomes, called genes, did their work.

While working with Boris Ephrussi at Caltech, Beadle conducted a series of experiments on the eye color of the fruit fly *Drosophilia melanogaster*. Beadle and Ephrussi proved that certain eye color mutations in the flies resulted from the turning off of certain genes that helped to produce the brown component of a fly's eye color. These experiments convinced Beadle that genes control the production of chemicals within cells.

At Stanford, Beadle continued to investigate this relationship with the chemist Edward L. Tatum and graduate student Joshua Lederberg. Together, they proved more specifically how genes control these chemical reactions. They showed that each gene produces a unique enzyme. These enzymes are then used by cells to conduct chemical reactions that help to determine many characteristics of how the cell operates, which in turn helps to determine how the organism that the cells compose grows and functions. In this way, genes help to determine each individual's unique characteristics.

Bibliography

Borek, Ernest. *The Code of Life*. New York: Columbia University Press, 1965.

Hoagland, Mahlon B. *Discovery: The Search for the DNA's Secrets*. Boston, Mass.: Houghton Mifflin, 1981.

McCarty, Maclyn. *The Transforming Principle: Discovering That Genes Are Made of DNA*. New York: W. W. Norton, 1985.

Paul Berg

Disciplines: Biology, cell biology, genetics, and virology

Contribution: Berg developed a technique to splice deoxyribonucleic acid (DNA) from different organisms. Splicing produces a tool for the study of chromosome structure and the biochemical basis of genetic disease via recombinant DNA technology.

June 30, 1926	Born in Brooklyn, New York
1944	Enters the U.S. Navy during World War II
1948	Graduates from Penn State University with a B.S. in biochemistry
1952	Receives a Ph.D. in biochemistry from Case Western Reserve University
1956	Becomes assistant professor of microbiology at Washington University Medical School
1959	Moves to Stanford University as an associate professor
1959	Receives the American Chemical Society's Eli Lilly Prize
1969-1973	Serves as chair of the biochemistry department at Stanford
1970	Named Wilson Professor of Biochemistry
1980	Receives the Nobel Prize in Chemistry
1983	Awarded National Medal of Science
1990	Becomes a trustee of Rockefeller University
1990	Chair of the advisory board of the Human Genome Project

Early Life

Paul Berg was born in Brooklyn to a clothing manufacturer, Harry Berg, and his wife Sarah. He attended city public schools including Abraham Lincoln High School, from which he graduated in 1943. There, Berg developed a strong interest in microbiology and biochemistry research. He credited much of this to Mrs. Wolf, who ran the school's science club.

Berg next entered Penn State University. His career plan, a degree in biochemistry, was interrupted by U.S. Navy service from 1944 to 1946. Afterward, Berg returned to Penn State. He married Mildred Levy in 1947 and had one son, John Alexander. In 1948, Berg graduated from Penn State with a B.S. in biochemistry.

Berg entered graduate school at Case Western Reserve University in Cleveland, Ohio. There, he was a National Institutes of Health (NIH) Fellow from 1950 to 1952. Berg received a Ph.D. in 1952.

After earning his Ph.D., Berg did postdoctoral work with Herman Kalckar at Denmark's Institute of Cytophysiology in Copenhagen and then with Arthur Kornberg at Washington University in St. Louis, Missouri. He stayed at Washington as a scholar in cancer research until 1957.

Splicing Genes

By 1956, Berg was an assistant professor of microbiology at Washington University. He left in 1959 to become an associate professor at Stanford University in California. During the 1950s Berg explored how amino acids, the building blocks (monomers) of proteins, become protein polymers via messenger ribonucleic acid (mRNA) and transfer ribonucleic acid (tRNA), members of a biomolecule class called nucleic acids.

Contemporary nucleic acid research had shown that mRNA and tRNA arise from the hereditary material deoxyribonucleic acid (DNA). DNA and RNA are huge polymers made of nucleotide subunits joined into long chains. Nucleotides contain components called bases in a genetic code. Base order (sequence) in DNA and RNA determines what each gene does.

Knowing this, Berg sought to combine genes from different species artificially, making "recombinant DNA." He reasoned that he could then study a gene from one species without interference encountered in original organisms, amid many neighboring genes. He began this work in the 1960s with simian virus 40 (SV40): a virus that infects monkeys and causes cancer.

By the 1970s, Berg had a gene map that showed where genes from SV40 were found in host cell DNA, their sequences, and what each one did. His work mixed SV40 genes with genes from monkeys, a virus called lambda, and the bacterium *Escherichia coli (E. coli)*. Berg performed this "cut and paste" by a method using restriction endonucleases and DNA ligation (splicing). For example, SV40 DNA and other DNAs are cut up into defined pieces with endonucleases. The pieces are then spliced to make recombinant DNAs, each of which contain one or several SV40 genes. Recombinant DNAs are next put into *E. coli* in order to make recombinant bacteria. Finally, the microbes are grown and the proteins made via SV40 genes are identified.

DNA, SV40, and Splicing

Genes from different organisms can be cojoined (spliced) in order to study chromosome structure and the biochemical basis of disease.

The flow of hereditary information can be simplistically stated as from deoxyribonucleic acid (DNA) to ribonucleic acid (RNA) to proteins. This Central Dogma of molecular biology, stated by Francis Crick, indicates that DNA is used to make messenger RNAs (mRNAs), each of which encode the production of a specific protein. Berg's Nobel Prize in Chemistry was given for two accomplishments. First was artificially combining genes from different species to make recombinant DNA. The other was sequencing and using the recombinant DNA to enable the study of individual genes from one species without interference found in the original organisms because of the presence of neighboring genes. This fundamental endeavor was based on the structure of DNA and on the availability of the enzymes (biological catalysts) that enabled Berg to cut and paste DNA into artificial constructs.

A DNA molecule, or chromosome, is composed of two DNA polymer strands, each made of conjoined subunits called nucleotides. Every nucleotide holds a sugar (deoxyribose), a phosphate, and one of four nitrogen-containing bases: adenine (A), cytosine (C), guanine (G), and thymine (T). The strands are actually two very long, intertwined polymer chains made up of chemically attached deoxyribose phosphate units. They are held together in ladderlike double helixes by interactions between bases that are found in pairs (such as AT), like ladder rungs.

This work led to an understanding of what each portion of SV40 DNA does, and it enabled work with genes from other organisms. Berg's research produced recombinant DNA technology. This aim of this technology includes making new organisms to suit societal needs; identifying the exact DNA sequence of all human genes, called the Human Genome Project; and curing human disease by inserting genes in molecules. Berg served as chair of the Human Genome Project in 1990. He chaired Stanford's biochemistry department from 1969 to 1974.

Part of Duplex with Bonds Broken by Chosen RE

...xxCTATAGxxxxxCTATAGxxxCTATAG...
...xxGATATCxxxxxGATATCxxxGATATC...

RE

...xxCTATA	GxxxxxCTATA	GxxxCTATA	G...
...xxG	ATATCxxxxxG	ATATCxxxG	ATATC...

DNA Fragments with Sticky Ends

A restriction endonuclease (RE) breaks part of a duplex into fragments with "sticky ends." Each x denotes an unspecified base in a nucleotide unit.

The base order (sequence) in some portions of a DNA strand determines the readout of the genetic code that is ultimately used to determine the sequence of amino acids present in a given protein (amino acid polymer) made by the cell. As bases match up in a fixed way—(A binds only to T, and G binds only to C)—the base sequence of a strand determines the sequence of the other strand, termed complementary, in the duplex.

Berg's experiments used as a probe DNA from simian virus 40 (SV40), which causes tumors in monkeys. He began by utilizing enzymes called restriction endonucleases (REs). An RE cuts a DNA duplex into fragments with defined single-stranded ends (see figure). These single-stranded ends can bind to other fragments that have complementary base sequences (for example, TATA can bind to ATAT), so they are called "sticky ends."

Berg worked most with SV40 DNA and the DNA of the bacterial virus (phage) lambda, which attacks the bacterium *Escherichia coli (E. coli)*. After he prepared SV40 and lambda fragments having sticky ends, Berg caused them to rejoin to produce lambda phage chromosomes, each containing one or a few SV40 genes. He then put the new recombinant chromosomes into *E. coli* by infecting these bacteria with the phage and studied new proteins produced by the bacteria that could only have come from SV40 genes. The production of SV40 proteins was caused by the use of SV40 DNA to make mRNAs producing specific proteins. Berg also sequenced the DNA fragments with which he worked.

Bibliography

Antebi, Elizabeth and David Fishlock. *Biotechnology: Strategies for Life*. Cambridge, Mass.: MIT Press, 1986.

Berg, Paul and S. P. Goff. "Construction of Hybrid Viruses Containing SV40 and Lambda Phage DNA Segments and Their Propagation in Cultured Monkey Cells." *Cell* 9 (1976).

Wade, Nick. *The Ultimate Experiment*. New York: W. H. Freeman, 1977.

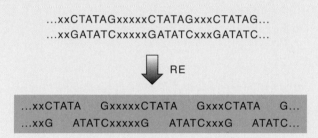

Altruism and the Nobel Prize

Berg recognized the danger of putting cancer genes in *E. coli*, which ubiquitously exist in sewage and the human body. Should recombinant bacteria escape laboratories, they could lead to huge rises in the incidence of cancer. Other laboratories, he feared, might also create dangerous recombinant organisms.

Consequently, Berg temporarily stopped his work and called together many other eminent scientists to discuss safeguards. Their dialogue, climaxing in a 1975 international meeting in Pacific Grove, California, outlined safeguards for federal regulations. Today, many such regulations, deemed unnecessary, have been relaxed. They might not have existed, however, without Berg's altruistic actions.

In 1980, Berg received the Nobel Prize in Chemistry for the fundamental study of nucleic acids and recombinant DNA. He also won other awards, such as an American Chemical Society's Eli Lilly Prize in 1959, the Lasker Medical Research Award in 1980, and the National Medal of Science in 1983. Berg was elected a member of the U.S. Academy of Arts and Sciences, France's Académie des Sciences, and Japan's Biochemistry Society. He was a trustee of Rockefeller University from 1990 to 1992. Throughout his career, Berg worked on recombinant DNA, including efforts to unravel the secrets of acquired immunodeficiency syndrome (AIDS).

Bibliography

By Berg

"An Enzymatic Mechanism for Linking Amino Acids to RNA," *Proceedings of the National Academy of Sciences*, 1958 (with E. J. Ofengand).

"Specificity in Protein Synthesis," *Annual Review of Biochemistry*, 1961.

"Biochemical Method for Inserting New Genetic Information into DNA of Simian Virus 40," *Proceedings of the National Academy of Sciences*, 1972 (with David A. Jackson and Robert H. Symons).

"Construction of Hybrid Viruses Containing SV40 and Lambda Phage DNA Segments and Their Propagation in Cultured Monkey Cells," *Cell*, 1976 (with Stephen P. Goff).

Genes and Genomes: A Changing Perspective, 1991 (with Maxine Singer).

Dealing with Genes: The Language of Heredity, 1992 (with Maxine Singer).

About Berg

Antebi, Elizabeth and David Fishlock. *Biotechnology: Strategies for Life*. Cambridge, Mass.: MIT Press, 1986.

Magill, Frank N., ed. "Paul Berg." in *The Nobel Prize Winners: Chemistry*. Pasadena, Calif.: Salem Press, 1990.

Wade, Nick. *The Ultimate Experiment*. New York: W H. Freeman, 1977.

(Sanford S. Singer)

Elizabeth Helen Blackburn

Disciplines: biological research, molecular biology

Contribution: Blackburn is noted for her discoveries on the genetic composition and function of telomeres. She co-discovered telomerase, the enzyme that replenishes the telomeres.

Nov. 26, 1948	Born in Hobart, Tasmania, Australia
1970	Earns B.S. in biochemistry at University of Melbourne
1972	Earns M.S. biochemistry at University of Melbourne
1975	Earns Ph.D. in molecular biology, University of Cambridge, England
1977	Completes postdoctoral work on molecular and cellular biology, Yale University
1981	Joins the faculty at the University of California, Berkeley
1990	Joins the faculty at University of California, San Francisco
1993	Becomes the first woman to head the UCSF School of Medicine, Department of Microbiology and Immunology
1998	Becomes president of the American Society for Cell Biology
2001	Awarded the Alfred P. Sloan Prize
2005	Awarded the Benjamin Franklin Medal in Life Sciences
2006	Receives the Albert Lasker Basic Medical Research Award
2009	Awarded the Nobel Prize in Medicine

Early Life

Elizabeth Blackburn, the second of seven children, was born in Hobart, the capital city of Tasmania (the island that forms the southernmost state in Australia). For the first four years of her life, she grew up in Snug, a tiny sea town near Hobart. Curious about animals, she would pick up ants in their backyard and jellyfish on the beach. Throughout her childhood, Blackburn was exposed to many pets, from canaries and goldfish to chickens and guinea pigs. Both of her parents were family physicians, and encouraged her interest in the science of living things.

Biology became an important interest, and as a teenager Blackburn decided to pursue science.

When she was in her teens, her family moved to Melbourne, and Blackburn attended her last year of high school at Melbourne's University High School, where one of her teachers further encouraged her interest in science.

Blackburn earned her bachelor's and master's degrees in biochemistry from the University of Melbourne in Australia, and was encouraged by her professors to continue her work at the University of Cambridge in England, where she became an expert in DNA sequencing. She completed her Ph.D. in molecular biology in 1975. After that, she pursued post-doctoral studies in molecular and cellular biology from 1975 to 1977 at Yale.

Research in California

In 1977, after completing her postdoctoral training, Blackburn moved to San Francisco, where her husband, John Sedat, had accepted a position as assistant professor at the University of California, San Francisco (UCSF). The university also offered Blackburn a research track position and space in the Department of Biochemistry in the genetics unit.

However, in 1978, Berkeley offered Blackburn an associate professor position in the Molecular Biology Department. Blackburn remained at the university until 1990.

Ethics Controversy

In 2002, Blackburn accepted an invitation to serve on President George W. Bush's Council on

Uncovering the Molecular Structure of the Telomere

Not much was known about telomeres when Blackburn arrived at Yale and began studying them in a one-celled organism, Tetrahymena, which she nicknamed "pond scum."

Telomeres are often compared to the plastic tips that keep the ends of shoelaces from fraying. Scientists had thought that telomeres protected the ends of chromosomes, but they did not know how the process worked. Blackburn deciphered the structure, finding that telomeres consisted of six DNA units, repeated many times.

Each time a cell divides, its telomeres shorten, but if they get too short, the cell cannot divide any more. However, in healthy cells, the telomeres are rebuilt. Blackburn and a researcher at Harvard University, Jack W. Szostak, determined that there must be an enzyme that keeps restoring the telomeres. Blackburn and her mentor, Joseph Gall, shared these findings in a landmark paper published in 1978, the same year that she joined the faculty of the University of California at Berkeley.

At Berkeley, Blackburn continued her work on telomeres. Her research suggested the existence of a unique enzyme that regulates the replication of the telomere, continuously rebuilding the ends of chromosomes to protect them in the cells of young organisms, and allowing them to decay in older ones. If its existence could be proved, and its mechanism understood, it would be the first step toward a new understanding of the aging process, of degenerative diseases in which healthy young cells suddenly die, and of cancer, where they multiply uncontrollably.

In 1984, Carol Greider, a graduate student in Blackburn's lab, found the enzyme—telomerase. Blackburn, Greider, and Szostak shared the Nobel Prize in Medicine in 2009. Until then, only eight women had won a Nobel Prize in medicine. It also was the first time two women had shared a Nobel science prize.

Bibliography

Grandin, Karl., ed. *Les Prix Nobel: Elizabeth Blackburn. The Nobel Prizes 2009*: Stockholm, Sweden: Nobel Foundation, 2010.

"Elizabeth Blackburn & Carol Greider: Deciphering the Puzzle of Human Aging," *Academy of Achievement, A Museum of Living History*, Washington, D.C., http://www.achievement.org/autodoc/page/bla0bio-1.

Bioethics. Supporting research using embryonic stem cells, she dissented from the views expressed by the president, the council's chairman, and the group's reports.

She was dismissed from council, although the Bush Administration and the head of the council insisted that her dismissal was not politically motivated. Blackburn said she believed the dismissal was political, and argued publicly that politics should not influence scientific advice. Much of the scientific world rallied around her.

Research Continues

Blackburn is the Morris Herzstein Professor of Biology and Physiology at UCSF, and a nonresident fellow of the Salk Institute. Her research team continues to explore the telomerase and telomere biology. Over the years, they have succeeded in more than doubling the life span of cells in the laboratory.

Bibliography

By Blackburn

"Identification of a Specific Telomere Terminal Transferase Activity in Tetrahymena Extracts, S In *Cell*, Vol. 43, No. 2, December 1985 (Part 1) pp. 405-413, January 1, 1985 (with Carol W. Greider).

About Blackburn

Brady, Catherine *Elizabeth Blackburn and the Story of Telomeres: Deciphering the Ends of DNA.* Cambridge, MA: MIT Press. 2007.

Grady, Denise. Profiles in Science, "Charting her own course," Science, The New York Times, April 8, 2013, http://www.nytimes.com/2013/04/09/science/elizabeth-blackburn-molecular-biologist-charts-her-own-course.html?pagewanted=all&_r=0

Death by Design/The Life and Times of Life and Times. Directed by Peter Friedman, 1995.

(Tsitsi D. Wakhisi)

Francis Crick

Disciplines: Biology, cell biology, and genetics

Contribution: Crick shared the Nobel Prize for his contributions in discovering the molecular structure of deoxyribonucleic acid (DNA) and devised the concept of the genetic code.

June 8, 1916	Born in Northampton, England
1934-1939	Studies at University College in London
1947	Awarded a grant to study biophysics at the Medical Research Council
1949	Begins work at the Medical Council Laboratory of Molecular Biology in Cambridge, England
1949-1953	Conducts graduate work in the laboratory of Max Perutz
1952	With James D. Watson, builds the double helix model of DNA
1953	Completes a Ph.D. in X-ray crystallography at Caius College, University of Cambridge
1953	Develops the idea of a universal genetic code
1959	Becomes Fellow of the Royal Society of London
1962	Named an honorary member of the American Academy of Arts and Sciences
1962	Shares the Nobel Prize in Physiology or Medicine
1977	Named J. W. Kieckhlefer Distinguished Research Professor at the Salk Institute for Biological Studies in La Jolla, California
1994-1995	Serves as president of the Salk Institute
July 28, 2004	Dies in San Diego, California

Early Life

Francis Harry Compton Crick was born on June 8, 1916, in Northampton, England. At an early age, Crick showed an interest in learning about the world. He wrote a magazine and distributed it to his family and friends. With the aid of a chemistry book, he performed experiments, including the making of small explosives, in his home.

At the age of fourteen, Crick began attending the Mill Hill School in north London, where he developed an affection for physics. He attended University College in London and graduated with a bachelor's degree in physics. As a graduate student there, he studied the effects of high pressure and temperature on water. During World War II, Crick left his graduate studies and worked in mine design for the British Admiralty, where he continued to work as a civilian after the war.

In 1947, Crick decided to return to graduate school. His graduate project at University College had been destroyed during the war, so he sought a different topic for his research. Molecular biology was a new field at the time, one that served Crick's interest in the mysterious border between the living and the nonliving.

He pursued this interest when he accepted a grant from the Medical Research Council to study biophysics. First, he studied tissue culture at the Strangeways Laboratory in Cambridge, England. Later, at the Cavendish Laboratory in Cambridge, he examined the structure of proteins using X-ray crystallography. This technique creates molecular pictures of the structures of large molecules using X-ray beams.

In 1949, Crick entered a doctoral program at Caius College, University of Cambridge, where he studied the structure of protein molecules. At that time, it was generally thought that protein molecules contained hereditary information. Crick suspected that deoxyribonucleic acid (DNA) also played a vital role in the storage of genetic information. His suspicions were shared by James D. Watson, an American postdoctoral fellow at the University of Cambridge.

The Double Helix

Crick met Watson in 1951. Crick had a superb knowledge of X-ray crystallography and protein structure. Watson, who had finished his Ph.D. at Indiana University in 1950, was knowledgeable on bacterial viruses and experimental design.

Between 1951 and 1953, these men shared an office and spent considerable time discussing DNA. Together, they studied X-ray crystallographs and assessed structural limitations for DNA. Much of the data that they studied came from work by Rosalind Franklin in the laboratory of Maurice H. F. Wilkins. Two key points simplified their work: a better understanding of the structure of nitrogenous bases and insight into how these bases create pairs. With this understanding, they used model building to develop their double helix model for DNA.

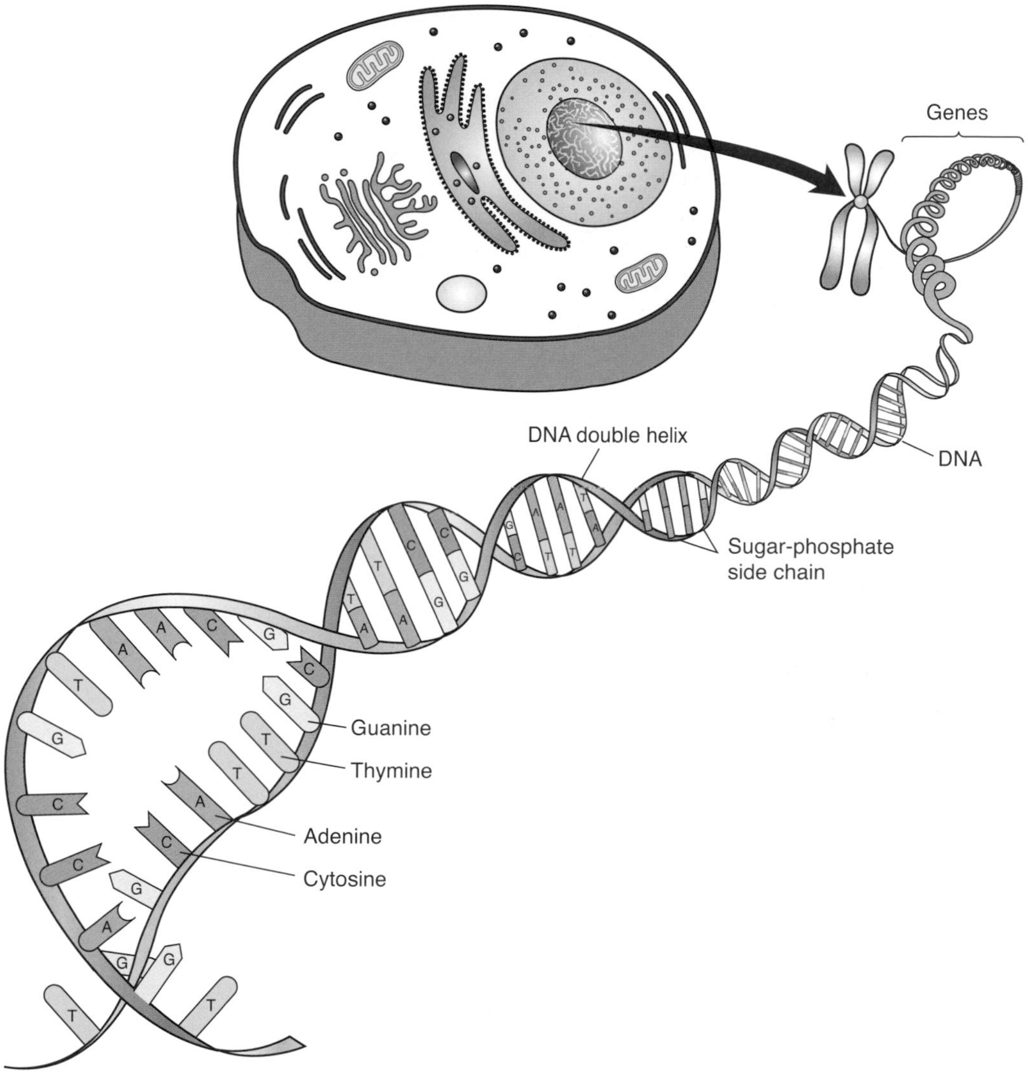

Crick and Watson published their discoveries in *Nature* on April 25, 1953. In 1962, Crick, Watson, and Wilkins won the Nobel Prize in Physiology or Medicine for "discoveries concerning the structure of nucleic acids and its significance for information transfer in living material." Franklin had died in 1958 and so was not included in the Nobel Prize, which cannot be awarded posthumously.

Even though Crick had contributed to one of the most significant scientific discoveries in molecular biology, he was still only a graduate student. In 1953 he completed his Ph.D. in protein structure.

The Genetic Code

During a brief period in 1953 while working at Brooklyn Polytechnic in New York City, Crick developed the idea of a universal genetic code for interpreting DNA instructions in the formation of protein molecules. As a member of the RNA Tie Club, a casual organization for scientists interested in the genetic code, he proposed the idea of adapter molecules that matched protein subunits with segments of ribonucleic acid (RNA). These molecules where later discovered and called transfer RNA (tRNA).

The Double Helix

Crick and Watson discovered the molecular structure of DNA and developed a model shaped like a double helix, which explained the concept of complementary base pairing and showed that DNA molecules are made from two polynucleotide chains.

All living things contain DNA, the molecule that stores genetic instructions for making protein. Eye coloring pigments, digestive enzymes, muscles, and hair fibers are some examples of components made from protein.

DNA is made of repeating units called nucleotides. Each nucleotide contains a phosphate molecule, a deoxyribose sugar molecule and a nitrogenous (nitrogen-containing) base. The only difference between nucleotides is the nitrogenous base that they contain: either adenine (A), thymine (T), cytosine (C), or guanine (G). A DNA molecule may contain thousands or even millions of nucleotides, each nucleotide having one of these four bases.

The nucleotides are attached to one another by bonds between the deoxyribose sugar of one nucleotide and the phosphate group of the next nucleotide to form a long chain called a polynucleotide. Crick and Watson showed that DNA molecules contained two polynucleotide chains.

In a polynucleotide, different nucleotides can be arranged to make instructions for creating any type of protein, just as the twenty-six letters of the alphabet can be arranged to make any word. The sequence of the nucleotides is vitally important to make clear instructions, just as the sequence of letters is important in understanding language.

Before the Watson-Crick model was developed, scientists were baffled by the equal amounts of adenine and thymine in DNA. Likewise, they could not explain why quantities of cytosine and guanine were the same. The Watson-Crick model shows how the nitrogen bases of the two polynucleotide chains are paired. Adenine is always paired with thymine, and cytosine always goes with guanine. These paired nitrogen bases are called complementary base pairs. Hydrogen bonds, a weak type of molecular attachment, hold the complementary base pairs together. These bonds also connect the polynucleotide chains.

The two polynucleotide chains joined by the hydrogen bonds between complementary base pairs form a structure similar to a twisted ladder. The deoxyribose sugars and phosphate groups of the nucleotides form the backbone or rails of the ladder, and the complementary base pairs held together by hydrogen bonds form the rungs of the ladder. The angles of the nucleotides cause the DNA ladder to be twisted; this twisted structure is called a double helix. There are ten nucleotides in each twist of the DNA double helix.

The double helix structure of DNA allows proteins and other molecules to interact with the DNA molecule. These interactions are important in understanding how DNA is copied and how changes in genetic material may occur.

Bibliography

Wilcox, Frank H. *DNA, the Thread of Life.* Minneapolis, Minn.: Lerner, 1988.

Genetics: Readings from "Scientific American." San Francisco, Calif.: W. H. Freeman, 1981.

Stent, Gunther S. *Molecular Genetics: An Introductory Narrative.* San Francisco, Calif.: W. H. Freeman, 1971.

Crick, F. H. C. "The Structure of the Hereditary Material." *Scientific American* 191 (October, 1954).

Crick returned to the University of Cambridge the following year and served as a faculty member until 1976. During this time, he aided in the formation of the so-called Central Dogma of molecular biology. The Central Dogma states that heritable information is stored in DNA and transferred to RNA, which is read during the formation of protein molecules.

Consciousness and the Soul

In 1977, Crick moved to San Diego, California, to study the brain at the Salk Institute for Biological Studies. His studies concentrated on the concept of consciousness through vision and the perception of visual images. He stayed in San Diego for the rest of his life, passing away in 2004.

Bibliography

By Crick

Of Molecules and Men, 1966.

Life Itself: Its Origin and Nature, 1981.

What Mad Pursuit: A Personal View of Scientific Discovery, 1988.

The Astonishing Hypothesis: The Scientific Search for the Soul, 1994.

About Crick

Watson, James D. *The Double Helix*. New York: New American Library, 1968.

Judson, Horace Freeland. *The Eighth Day of Creation*. New York: Simon & Schuster, 1979.

Magill, Frank N., ed."Francis Crick." in *The Nobel Prize Winners: Physiology or Medicine*. Pasadena, Calif.: Salem Press, 1991.

Sherrow, Victoria. *James Watson and Francis Crick*. Woodbridge, Conn.: Blackbrick Press, 1995.

(Beth Anne Short)

Jean Dausset

Disciplines: Genetics and immunology

Contribution: A pioneer in immunogenetic research, Dausset discovered the major histocompatibility complex in humans, a group of genes responsible for controlling tissue graft rejection.

Oct. 19, 1916	Born in Toulouse, France
1945	Earns an M.D. from the University of Paris
1946-1963	Directs the laboratories of the national blood transfusion center
1948	Awarded a Harvard Medical School Fellowship in hematology
1958	Teaches hematology at the University of Paris
1969	Officer in the French Legion of Honor
1969	Elected to the Belgian Royal Academy of Medicine
1977	Works as professor of experimental medicine at the Collège de France
1977	Elected to the Académie des Sciences
1978	Wins the Wolf Foundation Prize in Medicine
1979	Honorary member of the American Academy of Arts and Sciences
1980	Awarded the Nobel Prize in Physiology or Medicine
1984	Creates the Centre d'Études du Polymorphisme Humain (CEPH)
1993	CEPH becomes the Fondation Jean Dausset-CEPH

Early Life

Jean Baptiste Gabriel Joachim Dausset (pronounced "doh-SAY") was born in Toulouse, France, and went to high school at the Lycée Michelet in Paris. In the 1930s, he attended the University of Paris medical school before being drafted into the French army.

During World War II, Dausset was in North Africa fighting German troops with the Free French. Before going to North Africa, he helped a Jewish colleague at the Institut Pasteur hide from the Nazis by giving him his identity papers.

Blood Transfusions

In North Africa, Dausset worked in a resuscitation unit, where his experience in blood transfusions sparked an interest in immunohematology. Dausset left the army in 1945 and that same year, earned his M.D. from the University of Paris. In 1946, at only thirty, he became director of laboratories at the national blood transfusion center. Dausset then went to Harvard University in 1948 to study hematology and immunohematology for two years.

In the late 1940s, Dausset conducted extensive research on blood transfusions. In 1951, he discovered that strong immune (anti-A) antibodies could develop in type O blood from donors who had been vaccinated for diphtheria or tetanus. Up to that time, type O blood had been regarded as safe for individuals with all other blood types. Dausset's research initiated systematic blood testing for both donors and transfusion patients, thereby preventing dangerous reactions such as clotting.

The Immune System and Transplantation

In the 1950s, Dausset began a close study of the antibody phenomenon associated with blood disease and transfusion. In 1952, he published a paper that, for the first time, outlined how patients exposed to foreign tissue antigens through multiple transfusions subsequently produced antibodies against those introduced antigens.

Antigens are complex molecules that initiate and mediate antibody action in the immune system. This was the beginning of the definition of the human histocompatibility system: the immunogenetic complex that regulates successful tissue and organ transplantation according to whether tissues possess compatible antigens.

In 1958, Dausset outlined the human leukocyte antigen (HLA) system. This system is analogous to the major histocompatibility complex (MHC) that George D. Snell discovered in his transplantation research on mice in the 1940s and 1950s. The HLA complex that Dausset put forward is a genetically based system of antigens that can predict the compatibility of tissue transplants in humans. If a donor and recipient possess similar histocompatibility antigens on the surface of their tissue cells, the chance of successful transplantation becomes greater.

The Human Leukocyte Antigen Complex

Dausset discovered the human leukocyte antigen (HLA) complex, a genetic system responsible for controlling the cell surface antigens that provoke rejection of transplanted tissue.

"Histocompatibility" refers to a set of genes and the cell surface antigens that they control. In order to transplant tissues that will not be rejected, the histocompatibility antigens of the donor and the recipient must be similar. As a concept, histocompatibility refers to a condition or state in which the absence of immunological interference allows the grafting of tissue.

Through his work in blood diseases, Dausset discovered that a patient receiving multiple blood transfusions produced antibodies that reacted not with the antigens on the patient's own leukocytes (white blood cells) but with the antigens on the leukocytes from the donor's blood. Antibody-antigen binding, an immune function occurring at the molecular level, produces immunogens that cause particular immune responses that provide defenses against the invasion of microorganisms and foreign bodies.

In viewing successful blood transfusion as a type of tissue transplantation regulated by immune responses, Dausset saw a "bad" antibody-antigen reaction, which is what causes blood diseases, as a histocompatibility problem. This realization led to the description of the major histocompatibility system in humans.

In 1965, Dausset described a system containing approximately ten genetically programmed antigens. The appearance of these antigens on the surface of white blood cells is controlled by a group of various genetic sites located on the sixth chromosome. Dausset termed this immunogenetic system "Hu-1"; it is now called the human leukocyte antigen (HLA) complex. This complex is a major histocompatibility system, which means that it determines graft rejection according to the compatibility of specific transplantation antigens between donor and recipient.

For example, a kidney transplanted into the brother or sister of an HLA-identical donor has a nearly perfect success rate because no HLA incompatibilities occur. When HLAs differ, however, the foreign (dissimilar) antigens of a donor provoke a strong immune response from the recipient and cause the subsequent rejection of grafted tissue.

In terms of structure and function, Dausset's HLA complex is analogous to George D. Snell's major histocompatibility complex, which controls graft rejection in mice. This suggests that both mammalian systems evolved from a common genetic ancestry. In 1972, the HLA complex was shown to exist in fifty-four different human ethnic and racial populations, thereby proving that the genetic-based laws of the major human histocompatibility system not only have a common ancestry but also govern tissue rejection for all people. Along with the clinical evidence from hundreds of skin grafts, Dausset's population research established the immunogenetic law of human transplantation.

HLA research has had a significant impact on the understanding of the connection between immunogenetics and disease. Dausset investigated the relationship between acute lymphocyte leukemia and HLA in 1967. This research inspired other scientists to discover connections between the HLA system and juvenile diabetes, multiple sclerosis, rheumatoid arthritis, and other autoimmune diseases. Many scientists now believe that diseases may be prevented by identifying and manipulating a patient's HLA system.

Bibliography

Svejgaard, A. *The HLA System: An Introductory Survey*. Basel, Switzerland: S. Karger, 1979.

Klein, Ian. *The Natural History of the Major Histocompatibility Complex*. New York: John Wiley & Sons, 1986.

In the 1960s and 1970s, Dausset held international workshops on histocompatibility in order to organize and clarify the wide-ranging research that was being undertaken on HLAs. With Felix T. Rapaport, he initiated a program that performed hundreds of clinical skin grafts which proved that the genetically programmed HLA system is integral to tissue compatibility and, therefore, successful transplantation.

In 1966, Dausset served as one of the chairs of the International Tissue Transplantation Conference of the New York Academy of Sciences in order to spread the word that surgeons needed to conduct HLA-based donor screenings before transplantation surgery. He also helped to found the Transplantation Society in 1966 and acted as its secretary until 1970.

In 1980, Dausset won the Nobel Prize in Physiology or Medicine for discovering the fundamental role that the HLA system plays in tissue and organ transplantation. He shared the prize with George Snell of the Jackson Laboratory, and Baruj Benacerraf of Harvard Medical School.

Human Genome Mapping

In 1984, Dausset created the Centre d'Études du Polymorphisme Humain (CEPH), a research laboratory in Paris that specializes in molecular biology and genetics. The CEPH looks especially at the development of tools with which to analyze and construct maps of the human genome. In 1991, the CEPH and the AFM, the French muscular dystrophy association, created Généthon, a nonprofit research institute that provides tools to the scientific community for the isolation and cloning of disease-determining genes. In 1993, the CEPH was renamed the Fondation Jean Dausset-CEPH.

Bibliography

By Dausset

Immunohematologie biologique et clinique, 1956.

Tissue Typing, 1966 (as editor).

Advance in Transplantation: Proceedings of the First International Congress of the Transplantation Society, 1968 (as editor, with J. Hamburger and G. Mathe).

Human Transplantation, 1968 (with Felix T. Rapaport).

Histocompatibility Testing 1972, 1973 (with J. Colombani).

Histocompatibility, 1976 (with George D. Snell and Stanley Nathenson).

HLA and Disease, 1977 (as editor, with Arne Svejgaard).

Immunology 80: Fourth International Congress of Immunology, 1980 (as editor, with M. Fougereau).

"Tomorrow's Medicine (Must Confront AIDS Crisis Head-on)," *UNESCO Courier*, 1988.

"Our Genetic Patrimony," *Science*, 1994 (with Howard Cann).

"Scientific Knowledge and Human Dignity," *UNESCO Courier*, 1994.

About Dausset

Moritz, Charles., ed. *Current Biography Yearbook 1981*. New York: H. W. Wilson, 1981.

Marx, Jean L. "1980 Nobel Prize in Physiology or Medicine." *Science* 210 (November 7, 1980).

Clark, Matt. "A Nobel Piece of Research." *Newsweek* (October 20, 1980).

Dowie, Mark. *"We Have a Donor": The Bold New World of Organ Transplants*. New York: St. Martin's Press, 1988.

(Mark Gray Henderson)

Andrew Zachary Fire

Disciplines: Molecular biology and genetics
Contribution: Fire was awarded the Nobel Prize in Physiology or Medicine with Craig Mello for discovering how double-stranded RNA can switch off genes

April 27, 1959	Born Palo Alto, California
1978	Receives B.A. in mathematics at University of California, Berkeley
1983	Completes Ph.D. at Massachusetts Institute of Technology (MIT)
	Joins the Medical Research Council in Cambridge, England
1986	Joins the Carnegie Institution of Washington's Department of Embryology
2002	Awarded the Meyenburg Prize
2003	Joins Stanford University School of Medicine
	Receives the National Academy of Sciences Award
	Awarded the Wiley Prize in Biomedical Sciences
2004	Elected member National Academy of Sciences
2005	Receives Lewis S. Rosenstiel Award
	Receives the Gairdner Foundation International Award
2006	Receives the Paul Ehrlich and Ludwig Darmstaedter Prize
	Receives the Nobel Prize in Physiology or Medicine

Early Life

Born in 1959 at Stanford University Hospital, Frank Zachary Fire may be the only Nobel laureate to win the prize at the same institution where he was born. Fire, whose father was a Silicon Valley engineer, began his academic and scholarly journey in the public school system of Sunnyvale, California. He graduated from Fremont High School in 1975.

Although Stanford was his first choice, Fire attended the only other college he had applied to—the University of California, Berkeley, where he received a B.A. in mathematics in 1978. Fire immediately enrolled in the Ph.D. program in biology at the Massachusetts Institute of Technology (MIT) as a National Science Foundation Fellow.

At MIT, Fire was mentored by Nobel laureate geneticist Phillip Sharp. He completed the program in 1983 then trained for the next three years at the Medical Research Council Laboratory of Molecular Biology in Cambridge, England.

At Cambridge, he worked under yet another Nobel laureate, biologist Sydney Brenner, at the MRC Laboratory of Molecular Biology at Cambridge.

Fire moved to Baltimore in November 1986 and took a research position at the Carnegie Institution of Washington's Department of Embryology. With a research grant from the U.S. National Institutes of Health, he focused on DNA transformation technology.

In 2003, Fire moved back to Santa Clara County, taking a position at the Stanford University School of Medicine, where he currently holds the

RNA Interference (RNAi)

Fire and his associate, Craig C. Mello, worked with the Nematode C. elegans, *a tiny worm about the width of the lead in a No. 2 pencil. In these small, easily cultured worms they discovered a process called ribonucleic acid (RNA) interference, which allows cells to selectively turn off specific genes.*

At the root of genetic studies are questions of how a cell can distinguish "self" versus "nonself" and "wanted" versus "unwanted" gene expression. Before the RNA discovery, the scientific world thought proteins were the be-all and end-all for understanding how a cell operates. Fire and Mello discovered that it was RNA, not protein, which regulates the operation. Additionally, they discovered a natural means for switching off the flow of genetic information in the *Nematode C. elegans*, triggered by double-stranded RNA.

With RNA interference, the RNAs, so tiny that they are called microRNAs, stick to a certain RNA that is going to be made into protein. When the cell sees these two RNAs (double-stranded RNA) stuck together, the RNA cannot be translated into protein. Without RNA, there is no protein.

The discovery, made while Fire was at the Carnegie Institution's Department of Embryology in Baltimore, marked the first time that biologists were able to selectively "silence" the voice of one gene in the mix of the tens of thousands genes that are directing its life. By plucking out those that act abnormally with regard to the pathway in question, they are able to identify previously unknown genes involved in the pathway.

The discovery has helped scientists completely rethink the use of DNA in people, plants, and the animal kingdom. It allows scientists to study what genes do by controlling the method of switching genes off. RNAi-based treatments are being tested with such diseases as high cholesterol, HIV, cancer and hepatitis.

Bibliography

Greens, Kerry. "Fire and Mello win Nobel Prize: Researchers are honored for discovering the mechanism of RNA interference." *The Scientist*, October 2, 2006, http://www.the-scientist.com/?articles.view/articleNo/24394/title/Fire-and-Mello-win-Nobel-Prize/

"Shhhh: Silencing Genes with RNA Interference." *The Scientist*, April 2003, http://www.the-scientist.com/article/display/13678

"Andy Fire and Craig Mello win the Nobel Prize for their work on RNA interference thanks in part to the humble worm, C. elegans." *The Tech Museum of Innovation.* San Jose, Calif., http://genetics.thetech.org/original_news/news34

Nordqvist, Christian. "Nobel Prize In Medicine For Andrew Fire And Craig Mello," *Medical News Today*, Oct. 3, 2006, http://www.medicalnewstoday.com/articles/53323.php

Manus, M. T. M. and P. A. Sharp, "Gene silencing in mammals by small interfering RNAs." *Nature Reviews Genetics*, 3:737-47, October 2002.

title of Professor of Pathology and Genetics. Fire had been a professor at Stanford's Medical School for three years when he was awarded the Nobel Prize in Physiology or Medicine. He brought honor and prestige to the same university that 21 years earlier rejected his application for undergraduate admission.

Fire is a member of the National Academy of Sciences and the American Academy of Arts and Sciences. He also serves on the Board of Scientific Counselors and the National Center for Biotechnology, National Institutes of Health.

Bibliography

By Fire

"Integrative Transformation of Caenorhabditis-Elegans," *The EMBO Journal*, 1986.

"DNA transformation," *Methods in Cell Biology*, Volume 48: 451-582, 1995 (with Craig Mello).

"Potent and specific genetic interference by double-stranded RNA in Caenorhabditis elegans." *Nature*, 1998 (with Craig Mello et al.).

"Gene silencing by double-stranded RNA (Nobel Lecture)." *Angewandte Chemie*, 2007.

Cell autonomous specification of temporal identity by Caenorhabditis elegans microRNA," Developmental Biology, 2010 (with H. Zhang).

About Fire

Conger, Krista. "Andrew Fire shares Nobel Prize for discovering how double-stranded RNA can switch off genes." *Stanford School of Medicine*, October 4, 2006, http://med.stanford.edu/featured_topics/nobel/fire/

Grandin, Karl., ed. *Les Prix Nobel. The Nobel Prizes 2006*. Stockholm, Sweden: Nobel Foundation, 2007.

"Andrew Z. Fire - Biographical". Nobelprize.org. Nobel Media AB 2013. Web. 26 Sep 2013.

(Tsitsi D Wakhisi)

Rosalind E. Franklin

Disciplines: Biology, chemistry, genetics, and virology

Contribution: Franklin's measurement of deoxyribonucleic acid (DNA) fibers by diffraction were crucial to the model of DNA structure proposed by James D. Watson and Francis Crick.

July 25, 1920	Born in London, England
1941	Earns a bachelor's degree in physical chemistry from Newnham College, University of Cambridge
1941	Receives a fellowship to study with R.G. W. Norrish at Cambridge
1942	Works an assistant research officer of the British Coal Utilization Research Association
1945	Awarded a Ph.D. by Cambridge for her thesis on coal research
1947	Chercheur in the Laboratoire Central des Services Chimiques de l'État in Paris, working with Jacques Méring
1951	Receives a Turner-Newall Research Fellowship from King's College, University of Cambridge, to study with J. T. Randall
1953	Publishes a paper supporting the double helix model of DNA proposed by Watson and Crick
1953	Moves to the laboratory of Professor J. D. Bernal at Birkbeck College, University of London
Apr. 16,1958	Dies in London, England

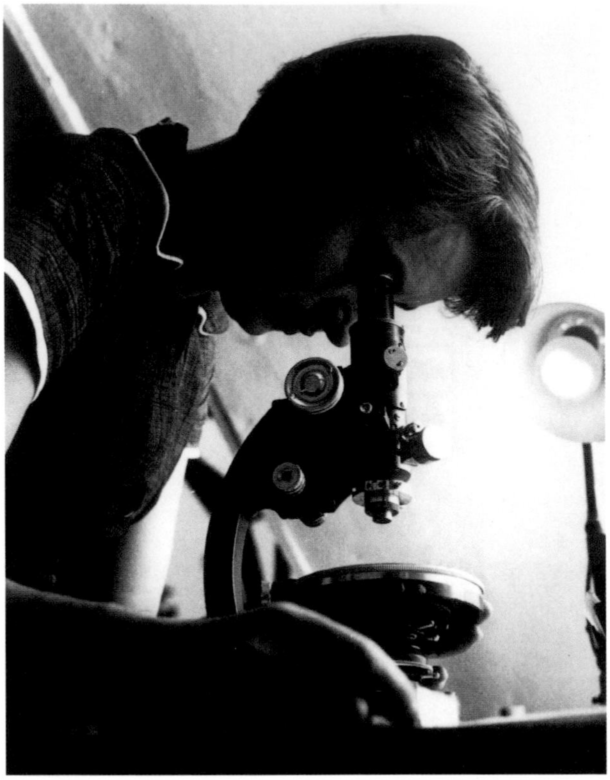

Early Life

Born on July 25, 1920, Rosalind Elsie Franklin was the second of five children in a wealthy Jewish family in London. Her keen intelligence and dedicated nature were recognized early and encouraged, although her decision at age fifteen to become a scientist was not wholly welcomed by her father.

Nevertheless, Franklin received an excellent education in the sciences at St. Paul's Girl's School in Hammersmith, London, and proceeded to Newnham College at the University of Cambridge, one of the few women's colleges of the time. Franklin was disappointed to receive only a high second-class degree (first class being the top), and she attributed this outcome to having worked herself to a state of exhaustion before the final examinations. Nevertheless, she was awarded a fellowship to continue graduate studies in physical chemistry under the noted chemist R. G. W. Norrish.

Physical Chemistry Research

In 1942, Franklin was appointed assistant research officer at the British Coal Utilization Research Association. While there, she was able to establish a reputation for painstaking and solid work in the physical chemistry of coal, while gathering data for a Ph.D. thesis. Her thesis, *The Physical Chemistry of Solid Organic Colloids with Special Relation to Coal and Related Materials* was published in 1945.

Franklin then moved to Paris, France, to work on the application of X-ray diffraction techniques to the elucidation of the structure of carbonaceous materials. She was named a chercheur (researcher) in the Laboratoire Central des Services Chimiques de l'État and conducted research with Jacques Mering.

The Switch to Biochemistry

Recognizing the growing importance of studying biological molecules, Franklin received a fellowship from King's College, University of Cambridge. She was charged with developing an X-ray diffraction unit in the laboratory of J. T. Randall that was devoted to determining the structure of deoxyribonucleic acid (DNA). Although she was uniquely suited to the difficult task of setting up the equipment and applying it to the awkwardly complex DNA molecule, Franklin found herself in an environment hostile to female scientists, and she came into conflict with her colleague Maurice H. F. Wilkins.

Nevertheless, Franklin succeeded in collecting X-ray diffraction images of DNA molecules and analyzing them correctly. Her data were essential to the construction of the double helix model of DNA proposed by James D. Watson and Francis Crick. She received little credit for her work, however, and was required to give up the DNA problem.

Too Short a Life

In 1951, Franklin moved to Birkbeck College, University of London, and the laboratory of

J. D. Bernal to pursue X-ray diffraction studies of the tobacco mosaic virus and other viruses. Between 1953 and 1958, she produced seventeen papers on this difficult subject, even though she had her first operation for cancer in 1956. Franklin died, at the age of thirty-seven, on April 16,1958.

The Nobel Prize in Physiology or Medicine was awarded to Watson, Crick, and Wilkins in 1962 for the elucidation of the structure of DNA. Nobel Prizes are not awarded posthumously.

Bibliography

By Franklin

"Molecular Configuration in Sodium Thymonucleate," *Nature*, 1953 (with R. G. Gosling).

"Evidence for 2-Chain Helix in Crystalline Structure of Sodium Deoxyribonucleate," *Nature*, 1953 (with Gosling).

"Location of the Ribonucleic Acid in the Tobacco Mosaic Virus Particle," *Nature*, 1956.

About Franklin

Bernal, J. D. "Dr. Rosalind E. Franklin." *Nature* 182 (July 1958).

Sayer, Anne. *Rosalind Franklin and DNA.* New York: Norton Library 1975.

(Lee Venolia)

The Determination of the Structure of DNA

X-ray diffraction analysis allowed key features of the three-dimensional structure of deoxyribonucleic acid (DNA) molecules to be determined.

X-rays have an appropriately small wavelength for producing interpretable diffraction patterns from molecular crystals. Their mathematical interpretation depends on the use of Fourier analysis and Patterson functions. While this interpretation can be straightforward for geometrical crystals, it is very complex for those biological molecules, such as DNA, that can be only partially crystallized.

Franklin determined that DNA appears in two distinct forms, depending on the level of hydration. The A form was the driest at 75 percent relative humidity. At higher humidities, a B form begins to appear, until it predominates. Earlier X-ray analysis was hampered by the complexity of this crystalline and paracrystalline mixture. Franklin took the first clear X-ray diffraction images of the B form, which is considered the biologically active form (although other forms, such as Z, are now recognized).

This image showed clearly that the B form molecule is a helix with an axial repeat of 34 angstroms and an axial spacing between nucleotides of 3.4 angstroms. The observation that the A to B change is reversible aided in the interpretation that the phosphate groups of the sugarphosphate backbone are on the outside of the helix.

Bibliography

Watson, J. D. et al. *Molecular Biology of the Gene.* 4th ed. Vols. 1 and 2. Menlo Park, Calif.: Benjamin/ Cummings, 1987.

Klug, A. "Rosalind Franklin and the Discovery of the Structure of DNA." *Nature* 219 (August, 1968).

Sir Francis Galton

Disciplines: Genetics, psychiatry, mathematics, astronomy

Contribution: Known for his studies of human heredity and intelligence and for originating the field called eugenics. He made significant contributions to meteorology and statistics.

Feb. 16, 1822	Born in Birmingham, England
1838	Begins medical studies at Birmingham General Hospital
1840	Interrupts his medical studies to read mathematics at the University of Cambridge
1844	Inherits sufficient wealth to be of independent means
1845-1852	Travels in Egypt, Sudan, Syria, Palestine, and southwest Africa
1856	Made a Fellow of the Royal Society of London
1863	Discovers the "anticyclone"
1866	Suffers a mental breakdown
1869	Publishes *Hereditary Genius*
1875	Publishes the first newspaper weather map
1883	Publishes *Inquiries into Human Faculty and Its Development*
1886	Awarded the Gold Medal of the Royal Society of London
1893	Establishes the importance of fingerprints in biological and criminal investigations
1904	Establishes the Eugenics Record Office at University College, London
Jan. 17, 1911	Dies in Haslemere, England

Early Life

Francis Galton, the youngest of seven surviving children of a Birmingham banker, was a half cousin of Charles Darwin. He was interested in science from an early age and began to study medicine at sixteen. He interrupted these studies to pursue mathematics at the University of Cambridge, where he suffered what was termed a nervous breakdown—Galton's long life was punctuated by severe depression.

His father's death in 1844 left him with a fortune, and thereafter he used his independent means to pursue his own interests. Galton never held or looked for paid employment. From 1845 to 1846 he traveled in Egypt, Palestine, and Syria. With the aid of the Royal Geographical Society, he financed and led an expedition from 1850 to 1852 to southwest Africa, hitherto uncharted.

On his return to England, his geographical work was recognized in scientific circles, and, in 1856 he was made a Fellow of the Royal Society of London.

With this appointment, Galton became a London-based scientist-at-large. In 1853, he married Louise Butler.

Galton always emphasized quantitative evidence, measuring and counting—indeed, his work indicates that he was obsessed with measurement. In 1863 he plotted meteorological data that led him to discover and name the "anticyclone." In 1875, he published in the first newspaper weather map in *The Times* (London).

Studies into Heredity

In the mid-1860s, when it became clear that his marriage was unlikely to result in children and following a nervous breakdown, Galton became interested in the work for which he is best known—human heredity and intelligence—and to which he devoted the latter part of his life. Galton was curious about the extent to which mental and physical characteristics depended on heredity or on environmental conditions, and so he became interested in selective breeding of plants and animals, and later of humans.

Galton advocated the application of scientific principles to human populations and claimed that people could be bred like animals to favor "desirable" traits and suppress unwanted ones.

Work such as *Hereditary Genius* (1869) led to the field that he called "eugenics" in his book *Inquiries into Human Faculty and Its Development* (1883). Eugenics refers to the intended improvement of the physical and mental makeup of the human species by selective parenthood.

Galton was convinced that preeminence in various fields was attributable almost entirely to hereditary factors, not to the environment. His ideas led him to advocate breeding restrictions to suggest seriously that "defective" people should not be allowed to reproduce and that those with "favorable" characteristics should be encouraged to have children. Galton inquired into racial differences and, like most Victorian intellectuals (including Karl Marx and Friedrich Engels) had decidedly politically incorrect views about women, Jews, and black people. He believed that his laboratory observations had demonstrated the intellectual inferiority of women.

Psychology

Galton was also an experimental psychologist and was one of the first to employ questionnaire and survey methods, which he used to investigate mental imagery in different groups of people. His work is fundamental to large areas of contemporary psychology, particularly to the fields of differential psychology and psychometrics. He was the first to investigate and measure individual differences in human abilities and traits. He provided evidence that such traits might be largely inherited in humans.

Statistics

His studies in heredity were hindered by shortage of quantitative information, so Galton began anthropometric research. Asking a question such as "How do the heights of parents relate to those of their children?" led Galton to collect intergenerational data on height and other characteristics. However, he faced the problem of how to express the extent to which heights of offspring varied as a function of the heights of the parents. He was the first to use the statistical technique of correlation to assess the relationship between measured qualities.

Although weak in mathematics, his ideas strongly influenced the development of statistics, particularly his proof that a normal mixture of normal distributions is itself normal. Another of his major findings was reversion, his formulation of regression, and its link to the bivariate normal distribution. In 1888, he presented to the Royal Society of London his technique for calculating correlation coefficients. Although it was crude, it was later improved by others.

Eugenics

Eugenics, which literally means "good genes" or "wellborn," may be regarded as the attempt to produce superior offspring.

The term "eugenics" applies equally to Plato's Republic and to Adolf Hitler's program of global extermination of all non-Caucasian and "deficient" humans. When Galton invented the term, as he wrote in *Inquiries into Human Vacuity and Its Development* (1883),

> he did so to have a brief word to express the science of improving the stock, which is by no means confined to questions of judicious mating, but which, especially in the case of man, takes cognizance of all the influences that tend in however remote a degree to give the more suitable races or strains of blood a better chance of prevailing speedily over the less suitable than they would otherwise have had.

"Positive" eugenics was intended to encourage the "fit" to have many children. "Negative" eugenics was to prevent the "unfit" from having children. Nazi "selection and eradication" initially focused on those whom eugenicists in Britain and the United States also wished to target—people who were physically disabled or mentally ill. Later, the Nazis sterilized and killed Jews, Gypsies, Slavs, and homosexuals, among others. The Nazi sterilization and killing programs drew on eugenic arguments and plans developed by scientists and politicians in Britain and the United States.

In the United States, eugenic concerns focused largely on ethnicity and race, and were used to justify social, ethnic, and racial prejudices. In 1907, states began to pass compulsory sterilization laws; by 1931, thirty states had such laws, usually directed at the "insane" and "feebleminded," categories often extended to include recent immigrants. By January, 1935, 20,000 people in the United States had been sterilized, mostly in California. From 1907 until the 1960s, more than 60,000 men and women were subjected to court-ordered, involuntary sterilization, often without their knowledge. Eugenics was also an intellectual force behind the legislation that outlawed interracial marriage.

Interest in eugenics generally decreased after World War II as a result of the abhorrence of Nazi practices. Past misuse of genetic information in Germany and the United States suggests the need for great caution in dealing with the genetic information that the Human Genome Project will provide. Threats of eugenic and genetic discrimination come substantially from the U.S. employment system, which is largely responsible for access to private health insurance and health care. The return of eugenics is evident in technologies such as artificial insemination, in vitro fertilization, embryo transfer, gene therapy, and fetal and anencephalic tissue transplantation.

Bibliography

Duster, Troy. *Backdoor to Eugenics*. New York: Routledge, 1990.

Holtzman, Neil A. and Mark A. Rothstein. "Eugenics and Genetic Discrimination." *American Journal of Human Genetics* 50, no. 3 (March, 1992).

Friedman, J. M. "Eugenics and the 'New Genetics." *Perspectives in Biology and Medicine* 35, no. 1 (Autumn, 1991).

Horgan, John. "Eugenics Revisited." *Scientific American* 268, no. 6 (June, 1993).

Neuhaus, Richard John. ed. *Guaranteeing the Good Life: Medicine and the Return of Eugenics*. Grand Rapids, Mich.: Wm. B. Eerdmans, 1990.

Garver, Kenneth L. and Bettylee Garver. "The Human Genome Project and Eugenic Concerns." *American Journal of Human Genetics* 54, no. 1 (January 1994).

Kevies, Daniel J. *In the Name of Eugenics: Genetics and the Uses of Human Heredity*. New York: Alfred A. Knopf, 1985.

Other Work

Galton was also instrumental in developing the fingerprinting technique used to identify criminals. He played a major role in the establishment of what became the Meteorological Office and the National Physical Laboratory. He was also influential in introducing geography as a subject at university level.

Galton established the Eugenics Record Office at University College, London, in 1904; it later became the Francis Galton Laboratory for the Study of Natural Eugenics. Galton was knighted in 1909. He died in 1911 and his will endowed the Chair of Eugenics at the University of London.

Bibliography

By Galton

Hereditary Genius: An Inquiry into Its Laws and Consequences, 1869.

Inquiries into Human Faculty and Its Development, 1883.

Memories of My Life, 1908.

Essays in Eugenics, 1909.

About Galton

Forrest, D. W. *Francis Galton: The Life and Work of a Victorian Genius.* New York: Taplinger, 1974.

Pearson, Karl. *The Life, Letters, and Labours of Francis Galton.* 3 vols. Cambridge, England: Cambridge University Press, 1914-1930.

Schwartz Cowan, Ruth. *Sir Francis Galton and the Study of Heredity in the Nineteenth Century.* New York: Garland, 1985.

(Maureen H. O'Rafferty)

Walter Gilbert

Disciplines: Cell biology, genetics, and physics

Contribution: Gilbert made crucial discoveries in molecular biology. He isolated the *lac* repressor and was one of the scientists who discovered the molecular structure of genes.

Mar. 21, 1932	Born in Boston, Massachusetts
1957	Earns a Ph.D. in mathematics from the University of Cambridge
1959	Becomes assistant professor in physics at Harvard University
1968	Becomes professor of biochemistry at Harvard
1968	Becomes a member of the American Academy of Arts and Sciences
1968-1969	Receives a Guggenheim Fellowship
1972-1981	Works as the American Cancer Society Professor of Molecular Biology at Harvard
1978-1983	Becomes Chair of the Scientific Board of Directors of Biogen N.V.
1979	Receives the Albert Lasker Basic Medical Research Award
1980	Awarded the Nobel Prize in Chemistry
1987	Becomes a Member of the Royal Society of London
1987	Appointed Carl M. Loeb University Professor at Harvard
1992	Becomes vice chair of Myriad Genetics, Inc.
1996	Founds Paratek Pharmaceuticals
2001	Becomes Partner of BioVentures Investors

Early Life

Walter Gilbert was born on March 21, 1932, in Boston, Massachusetts, where his father was a professor of economics at Harvard University. His mother, Emma Cohen, was a child psychologist who first educated Gilbert and his sister at home, instilling in Gilbert a love of reading. Gilbert would later skip classes in Washington, D.C., where the family moved in 1939, to go to the Library of Congress and read about atomic physics.

At Harvard University, Gilbert majored in physics and chemistry. After a year in graduate school at Harvard, he moved to the University of Cambridge, England where, in 1957, he received a Ph.D. in mathematics. His thesis supervisor was Abdus Salam, a later Nobel laureate. Although Gilbert returned to Harvard as a physicist, he soon shifted to molecular biology and was encouraged by James D. Watson, the codiscoverer of the molecular structure of deoxyribonucleic acid (DNA).

Gene Regulation and the *Lac* Repressor

In molecular biology, Gilbert started to work on one of the central topics: the question of how genes are turned on and off in a living cell. In 1966 together with Benno Müller-Hill, he isolated the *lac* repressor, a protein that binds to the area of DNA carrying the gene for the enzyme that digests lactose, thus preventing this gene from being expressed. This discovery was a crucial piece of evidence in support of the famous model of gene regulation first proposed by François Jacob and Jacques Lucien Monod.

DNA Sequencing and the Nobel Prize

The discovery of the *lac* repressor motivated Gilbert to work on chemical sequencing of DNA, work for which he was eventually awarded the Nobel Prize in Chemistry, which he shared with Frederick Sanger and Paul Berg. Initially, the binding of the *lac* repressor to a specific region of DNA allowed him to isolate this fragment and determine its sequence by chemically breaking it into smaller pieces.

In the 1970s Gilbert and his associates improved sequencing technology and later advocated its large-scale use in the Human Genome Project, an international effort to determine the sequence of the entire human genome. Gilbert also developed some of the recombinant DNA techniques necessary for the production of mammalian gene products, such as insulin, in bacteria.

The Structure of Genes

DNA sequencing led to insights into the molecular structure of genes. Gilbert and his colleagues detected an important difference in the structure of bacterial genes and genes of higher organisms. While bacterial genes consist of an uninterrupted strain of codons, genes of higher organisms are composed of a series of codons interrupted by noncoding DNA. Only the coding elements contribute to the final gene product—the protein.

Basic Science and Commercial Application

Gilbert was always an advocate for the practical application of basic research. In 1978, he helped to found the genetic engineering company Biogen N.V., which produced the human antiviral substance interferon using recombinant DNA technology. From 1981 to 1984, he took leave from academic science and served as principal executive officer of Biogen N.V. In 1992, Gilbert founded Myriad Genetics, Inc., a private company involved in the efforts to sequence the human genome.

Bibliography

By Gilbert

"Molecular and Biological Characterization of Messenger RNA," *Cold Spring Harbor Symposia*, 1961 (with François Gros et al.).

"Isolation of the Lac-Repressor," *Proceedings of the National Academy of Sciences*, 1966 (with B. Müller-Hill).

"Why Genes in Pieces?," *Nature*, 1978.

"DNA Sequencing and Gene Structure," *Science*, 1981.

"Genomic Sequencing," *Proceedings of the National Academy of Sciences*, 1984 (with G. Church).

About Gilbert

Encyclopædia Britannica Online, s. v. "Walter Gilbert," accessed September 27, 2013.

James, Laylin K., ed. *Nobel Laureates in Chemistry, 1901-1992*. Washington, D.C.: American Chemical Society, 1993.

Magill, Frank N., ed. *The Nobel Prize Winners: Chemistry*. Pasadena, Calif.: Salem Press, 1990.

(Manfred D. Laubichler)

The Structure of Genes

Genes of higher organisms are composed of pieces of coding deoxyribonucleic acid (DNA), the exons, separated by pieces of noncoding DNA, the introns.

The development of DNA sequencing technology by Gilbert and his colleagues allowed them to characterize the molecular structure of genes. They found an important difference between bacterial genes and the genes of higher organisms. Bacterial genes consist of a continuous series of codons, or information-carrying pieces of DNA, that lie between an initiation signal and a termination signal. The information of such a bacterial gene is directly transcribed into a messenger ribonucleic acid (mRNA) and then translated into a protein.

In higher organisms, the information-containing elements of the DNA, the exons, are separated by noncoding elements, the introns. Before the genetic information can be translated into a protein, the initial RNA transcript has to be edited. A variety of molecular mechanisms are now known to contribute to this edited process.

This fragmented structure of genes has important evolutionary consequences. Separating the exons of a single gene allows for higher rates of recombination and therefore more evolutionary flexibility. In addition, Gilbert and his coworkers estimated that only 1,000-7,000 original exons were needed to derive all known genes by means of different combinations of exons. This would explain how the enormous variation in genes could originate during evolution.

Bibliography

Solomon, Eldra Pearl et al. *Biology*. Fort Worth, Tex.: Saunders College Publishing, 1996.

Gilbert, Walter, Robert L. Dorit, and Lloyd Schoenbach. "How Big Is the Universe of Exons?" *Science* 250 (December 7, 1990).

Carolyn Widney Greider

Disciplines: Molecular biology
Contribution: Codiscovered telomerase, a key enzyme in cancer and anemia research, and pioneered research on the structure of telomeres, the protective ends of the chromosomes.

April 15, 1961	Born in San Diego, California
1983	Receives B.A. in biology from the University of California, Santa Barbara
1987	Completes Ph.D. at the University of California, Berkeley
1998	Receives the Gairdner Foundation International Award
1999	Elected to the American Society for Cell Biology
2000	Receives the Academy of Achievement Golden Plate Award
2003	Elected to the American Academy of Arts and Sciences
	Elected to the National Academy of Sciences
	Receives the Richard Lounsbery Award
2004	Elected to the American Society for Biochemistry and Molecular Biology
2009	Awarded the Nobel Prize in Physiology or Medicine
	Awarded the Paul Ehrlich and Ludwig Darmstaedter Prize
2010	Elected to the Institute of Medicine

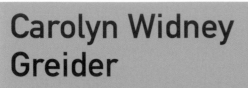

Early Life

Carolyn Widney Greider, known as Carol, was born in 1961 into a scientific household in San Diego. Her father, Kenneth Greider, had a Ph.D. in physics, and her mother, Jean Foley Greider, had a Ph.D. in botany.

A year after their daughter's birth, the Greiders moved to New Haven, Connecticut, where Kenneth Greider accepted a faculty position in the physics department at Yale, and Jean Foley Greider took a postdoctoral position at a Yale laboratory, where she worked on fungal species.

In 1965, the family returned to California after Greider's father took a faculty position in the physics department at the University of California, Davis. Her mother taught at a Sacramento community college and later at American River College.

Two years after the family returned to California, Greider's mother died. As hard as this was for the family, Greider later stated that her mother's death led her to learn how to do things on her own at an early age.

Greider struggled in elementary school. Unable to sound out words phonetically, she was put in remedial spelling classes and assigned a special teacher who came weekly to give her special spelling lessons. Greider was embarrassed for being singled out for remedial work. She did not realize until later that she was actually dyslexic.

In 1971, the family moved to Germany for a year when Kenneth Greider was invited to take his sabbatical at the Max Planck Institute for Nuclear Physics in Heidelberg.

Greider said her grades continued to suffer at the Englisches Institut, a private school. She would routinely receive D's and F's in English because of misspelled words. Nevertheless, she became fluent in German. When the family returned to California, Greider, now in sixth grade, began to make improvements in her schoolwork. Instead of sounding out words, she memorized them. Soon she was receiving high grades.

She graduated from Davis Senior High School in 1979, and with an interest developed in high school for biology, she headed to the University of California, Santa Barbara. She graduated four years later in 1983.

Telomere Terminal Transferase

Greider joined Elizabeth Blackburn's laboratory in April 1984, at the University of California, Berkeley, where she was pursuing a Ph.D. The two worked on finding the enzyme that was hypothesized to add extra DNA bases to the ends of chromosomes. Without the extra bases, chromosomes are shortened during DNA replication, eventually resulting in chromosome deterioration and senescence or cancer-causing chromosome fusion.

Blackburn and Greider looked for the enzyme in the model organism *Tetrahymena thermophila*, a freshwater protozoan with a large number of telomeres.

On Christmas Day, 1984—only a year out of college—Greider first obtained results indicating that she had found the responsible enzyme. An additional six months of research led Greider and Blackburn to the conclusion that they had, indeed, identified the enzyme responsible for telomere addition, for which they would later earn a Nobel prize. They published their findings in the journal *Cell* in December 1985. The enzyme, originally called "telomere terminal transferase," is now known as telomerase.

In the absence of telomerase, telomeres shorten progressively as cells divide, and telomere function is lost. For this reason, telomerase is required for cells that undergo many rounds of divisions, especially tumor cells and some stem cells.

In her own words, Greider explains what she learned from her collaboration with Blackburn: "Mostly, I learned the importance of questioning your own assumptions. We did not set out to prove we had a new enzyme, rather we imagined all the ways our own thinking could be deceiving us and allowing us to interpret our results in a way that favored our bias."

Bibliography

"Carol W. Greider - Biographical". Nobelprize.org. Nobel Media AB 2013. Web, September 3, 2013. http://www.nobelprize.org/nobel_prizes/medicine/laureates/2009/greider-bio.html

Mundy, Liza "Success is in her DNA," *Washington Post*, Oct. 20, 2009, http://articles.washington-post.com/2009-10-20/news/36827497_1_jack-szostak-telomeres-carol-greider

Post Telomerase Discovery

Greider completed her Ph.D. in molecular biology in 1987 at the University of California, Berkeley, under Elizabeth Blackburn. She then completed her postdoctoral work, and also held a faculty position at the Cold Spring Harbor Laboratory, Long Island, New York. During this time, Greider, in collaboration with Ronald A. DePinho, produced the first telomerase knockout mouse, showing that short telomeres result in premature aging.

At The Johns Hopkins University, where she became the director of molecular biology and genetics at the Johns Hopkins Institute of Basic Biomedical Sciences, Greider and her colleagues continue to study telomerase, which has had major impact on the understanding and treatment of cancer and anti-aging related diseases.

Honors and Recognition

Greider has been highly regarded in the scientific community and has been recognized for her contributions to science on many occasions. She has been elected to American Society for Cell Biology, the National Academy of Sciences, and the Institute of Medicine. Greider has also received the Richard Lounsbery Award, The Gold Plate Award, the Dickson Prize in Medicine, and the Paul Ehrlich and Ludwig Darmstaedter Prize. Perhaps her most famous recognition came in 2010, when she, along with Elizabeth Blackburn and Jack W. Szostak, were awarded the Nobel Prize in Physiology or Medicine for the discovery of how chromosomes are protected by the telomeres and the enzyme telomerase.

Bibliography

By Greider and Blackburn

"Identification of a specific telomere terminal transferase activity in Tetrahymena extracts," Cell 43 (2 Pt 1): 405-13. December 1985 (with Elizabeth Blackburn).

"Telomeres, Telomerase and Cancer," Scientific American: 92–97, February 1996, and reprint at Scientific American, October 5, 2009: http://www.scientificamerican.com/article.cfm?id=telomeres-telomerase-and (with Elizabeth Blackburn).

Molecular Biology: Principles of Genome Function, 2010 (with Nancy Craig et al.).

About Grieder

Nuzzo, Regina. "Biography of Carol W. Greider." *The National Academy of Sciences*, 2005.

"Carol W. Greider – Biographical." Nobelprize.org. Nobel Media AB 2013. Web, September 2013, http://www.nobelprize.org/nobel_prizes/medicine/laureates/2009/greider-bio.html

Dreifus, Claudia "A Conversation With Carol W. Greider On Winning A Nobel Prize in Science," *New York Times*, October 13, 2009, http://www.nytimes.com/2009/10/13/science/13conv.html (Accessed June 15, 2011)

(Tsitsi D. Wakhisi)

J. B. S. Haldane

Disciplines: Biology, genetics, and physiology
Contribution: Haldane provided new ideas and supporting research in respiratory physiology, chromosome mapping, sex linkage, and enzyme physiology.

Nov. 5, 1892	Born in Oxford, England
1914	Graduated from Oxford University in classical studies
1919	Elected a Fellow of New College, Oxford
1923	Appointed Sir William Dunn Reader in Biochemistry at the University of Cambridge
1933	Chair of genetics at University College, London
1937	Appointed to the Weldon Chair of Biometry at University College
1937	Joins the Spanish Civil War effort and becomes science correspondent, and later an editor, for the communist *Daily Worker*
1938	Publishes *Heredity and Politics* discrediting Nazi genetic superiority theories
1940	Conducts experiments on gas levels for escape from submarines
1957	Accepts a research professorship at Indian Statistical Institute in Calcutta
1961	Heads research unit of Council of Scientific and Industrial Research in India
1962	Director of Genetics and Biometry Laboratory, Bhubaneswar, India
Dec. 1, 1964	Dies in Bhubaneswar, India

Early Life

John Burdon Sanderson Haldane was born in Oxford, England, on November 5, 1892. The young Haldane was influenced by his father, physiology professor John Scott Haldane, who often took his son along when investigating mine explosions. Haldane entered the University of Oxford, pursuing the classical curriculum and graduating with honors.

On the eve of World War I, Haldane enlisted in the Black Watch and soon he discovered his talent for necessary risk-taking. He fought in trench warfare in France and was wounded in Mesopotamia. Haldane recuperated in India and became the director of a bombing school there.

Academic Career

After the war, Haldane returned to New College at Oxford to begin his scientific work. Haldane became head of genetics at John Innes Horticultural Institution in 1925.

In 1933, he accepted the chair of genetics at University College in London. He was appointed Weldon Chair of Biometry there in 1937. In 1957, he resigned and immigrated to India, serving at the Indian Statistical Institute in Calcutta and the Council of Scientific and Industrial Research. In 1962, he directed the Genetics and Biometry Laboratory in Bhubaneswar, India, where he died in 1964.

Research

In the new science of genetics, Haldane made major contributions to understanding gene linkages in organisms with more than standard paired chromosomes, called polyploids. This research required development of new mathematical techniques, and Haldane was skilled at biometry. His ten papers published between 1924 and 1934 made evolution a quantitative science by measuring the rate of genetic change over time. Haldane's extensive knowledge of physiology and biochemistry allowed him to extend the relationships of genes to the working of an actual organism, and especially to its survival over time through evolution.

Beyond what he could study in detail, Haldane posed questions for future researchers. His speculation about the conditions and properties of the first life on Earth, called the Oparin-Haldane hypothesis, is still found in textbooks.

Kin Selection

Haldane casually wrote about the advantage to an individual of possessing a gene for saving a relative from drowning, if the risk of drowning while performing this act was low. This concept, today called "kin selection," was not proven mathematically until William Hamilton did so decades later.

Measuring the Rate of Evolution

Research had already established that natural selection could cause a species to change over time. Haldane set out to show how the rates of genetic change could be measured to account for past, present, and future populations.

In the first of ten papers on "The Mathematical Theory of Natural and Artificial Selection," Haldane presented thirteen scenarios and provided the necessary formulas to predict the evolutionary rate of change in these populations. In the simplest case, a gene is dominant and will express itself when it is inherited with another gene. If it has a very slight selective advantage over the other gene, how fast will the dominant gene increase in the population over time?

Haldane's formulas showed that it would take 6,920 generations to move from 0.001 percent of the population to 1 percent. Only 4,819 more generations would be required for the gene to occur in 50 percent of the population. In another 11,664 generations, the gene would be found in 99 percent of the members, but it would take 309,780 generations to push the gene to 99.999 percent.

In the twelve papers that followed, Haldane pursued such mathematical rates of evolution in self-fertilization, inbreeding, isolated populations, and other real situations. Haldane's book, *The Causes of Evolution* (1932), became famous for this mathematical analysis of evolution.

Bibliography

Haldane, J. B. S. *The Causes of Evolution.* London: Longmans, Green, 1932.

Dronamraju, Krishna R., ed. *Haldane and Modern Biology.* Baltimore, Md.: The Johns Hopkins University Press, 1968.

By the end of his life, Haldane had written twenty-three books, more than 400 scientific papers, and uncounted popular science articles.

Popularization for the People

Having experienced gas warfare in World War I, Haldane wrote a provocative defense of chemical warfare called *Callinicus* (1925) that compared it to far more inhumane shrapnel. Haldane was a Communist Party member from 1942 onward. He wrote a weekly column popularizing scientific concepts in the *Daily Worker*.

Haldane's columns and the books collecting his essays made him England's most widely read "pop scientist." Author Aldous Huxley, a family friend, drew the idea of artificial procreation in the novel *Brave New World* (1932) straight from Haldane's speculations. Essays such as "On Being the Right Size" offered new perspectives and posed questions that science had not before addressed—and they first appeared in a communist newspaper.

Because Haldane had conducted vital submarine rescue research for the Admiralty, his loyalty was unquestionable. Nevertheless, because of his party membership, he was restricted in research in England and was denied speaking invitations in the United States.

Bibliography

By Haldane

Daedalus: Or, Science and the Future, 1923.
Callinicus: A Defence of Chemical Warfare, 1925.
Animal Biology, 1927 (with J. S. Huxley).
Possible Worlds and Other Essays, 1927.
Enzymes, 1930.
The Causes of Evolution, 1932.
The Inequality of Man and Other Essays, 1932.
Biology in Everyday Life, 1934 (with J. R. Baker).
The Outlook of Science, 1935.
Science and the Supernatural, 1935 (with A. Lunn).
My Friend, Mr. Leakey, 1937.
Heredity and Politics, 1938.
The Marxist Philosophy and the Sciences, 1938.
Science and Everyday Life, 1939.
Science in Peace and War, 1940.
Keeping Cool and Other Essays, 1940.
New Paths in Genetics, 1941.
A Banned Broadcast and Other Essays, 1946.
Science Advances, 1947.
What Is Life?, 1947.
Everything Has a History, 1951.
The Biochemistry of Genetics, 1954.
The Unity and Diversity of Life, 1958.

About Haldane

Dronamraju, Krishna R., ed. *Haldane's "Daedalus" Revisited.* Oxford, England: Oxford University Press, 1995.
Clark, Ronald William. *J. B. S.: The Life and Work of J. B. S. Haldane.* New York: Coward-McCann, 1968.
Gardner, Martin. "The Sad Story of Professor Haldane." *Skeptical Inquirer* (1992).

(John Richard Schrock)

Alice S. Huang

Disciplines: Genetics, medicine, and virology

Contribution: Huang's research on viral genetics aided in the discovery of the enzyme reverse transcriptase. She also studied how abnormal viruses interfere with the reproduction of normal viruses.

Mar. 22, 1939	Born in Nanchang, Jianxi, China
1949	Immigrates to the United States
1957-1959	Attends Wellesley College
1959-1966	Attends The Johns Hopkins University, earning bachelor's, master's, and Ph.D. degrees
1966	Employed as a visiting assistant professor at the National Taiwan University
1967	Serves a postdoctoral fellowship at the Salk Institute
1968-1969	Serves postdoctoral fellowship at the Massachusetts Institute of Technology (MIT)
1969-1970	Employed as a research associate at MIT
1970	Works as lecturer at the National Taiwan University
1971-1978	Serves as an assistant and then associate professor at Harvard University
1975	Shares the Nobel Prize for Physiology or Medicine
1977	Receives the Eli Lilly Award
1979-1991	Employed as a professor at Harvard
1988-1989	Serves as president of the American Society for Microbiology
1991	Appointed the dean of science at New York University

Early Life

Alice Shih-hou Huang was born in Nanchang, China, on March 22, 1939. Her parents were Quentin K. Y. Huang, a bishop in the Anglican Episcopal Church, and Grace Betty Soong Huang, a nurse.

In 1949, when the Communist Party took control of the government of China, Alice and her siblings were sent to live in the United States. She studied at an Episcopal boarding school in Burlington, New Jersey, and at the National Cathedral School in Washington, D.C. Huang became a citizen of the United States while a senior in high school.

Huang attended Wellesley College, in Massachusetts, from 1957 to 1959. She then enrolled at the School of Medicine at The Johns Hopkins University in Baltimore, Maryland, where she earned a bachelor's degree in 1961, a master's degree in 1963, and a Ph.D. in 1966. In 1966, she served as a visiting assistant professor at the National Taiwan University in Taipei.

Huang served as Dean of the Faculty of Science at NYU.

Postdoctoral Research

After returning to the United States, Huang began working with David Baltimore as a postdoctoral fellow at the Salk Institute for Biological Studies in San Diego, California. The two virologists were married in 1968. That same year, they took their research to the Massachusetts Institute of Technology (MIT), where Huang continued to serve as a postdoctoral fellow.

Huang's study of viral genetics enabled the discovery of the enzyme reverse transcriptase, which is involved in the reproduction of viruses known as retroviruses. For this discovery, Baltimore shared the 1975 Nobel Prize for Physiology or Medicine with Renato Dulbecco and Howard M. Temin.

The Harvard Years

Huang worked as a research associate at MIT from 1969 to 1970, then returned to the National Taiwan University in 1970 as a lecturer. In 1971, she began her career at the Medical School of Harvard University as an assistant professor. She was promoted to associate professor in 1973 and to professor in 1979.

Huang's research at Harvard involved abnormal viruses known as defective interfering particles, which block the reproduction of normal viruses. For this research, she was granted the Eli Lilly Award in Microbiology and Immunology in 1977. From 1988 to 1989, she served as president of the American Society of Microbiology. Huang left Harvard in 1991 to serve as dean of science at New York University.

While working at Harvard, Huang also served as a scientific associate at Boston City Hospital, a visiting associate professor at Rockefeller University in New York, and a visiting professor at the University of Mississippi.

Defective Interfering Particles

Defective interfering particles are abnormal viruses that interfere with the reproduction of normal viruses and that appear to he involved in determining the patterns of viral infections.

A normal virus consists of a chain of deoxyribonucleic acid (DNA) or ribonucleic acid (RNA) within a protein shell. Viruses must invade living cells within other organisms to reproduce. An invading virus uses the host cell's internal biological mechanisms to make copies of the viral DNA or RNA. These copies cause the host cell to produce the proteins that make up the viral shell. The DNA or RNA combines with the proteins to form new viruses.

Occasionally, an abnormal virus is produced during this process. This virus, known as a defective interfering particle, consists of a normal protein shell surrounding a small part of the viral DNA or RNA. The particle is able to reproduce itself only when normal viruses are present.

As more defective interfering particles are produced, fewer normal viruses are produced. Eventually, the number of normal viruses is low enough that the number of defective interfering particles declines also. If the host is able to destroy the few remaining viruses, the disease is limited. If the remaining viruses survive to cause a new infection, the disease is recurrent.

Bibliography

A Dancing Matrix: Voyages Along the Viral Frontier. Robin Marantz Henig. New York: Alfred A. Knopf, 1993.

An Introduction to Virology. Clyde R. Goodheart. Philadelphia: W. B. Saunders, 1969.

Introduction to Virology. K. M. Smith and D. A. Ritchie. London: Chapman and Hall, 1980.

Huang also served as a laboratory director at the Children's Hospital in Boston. She was an associate editor of *Reviews of Infectious Diseases* and on the editorial boards of *Intervirology*, *Archive of Virology*, *Journal of Virology*, and *Microbial Pathogenesis*.

Bibliography

By Huang

"Defective Viral Particles and Viral Disease Processes," *Nature*, 1970 (with David Baltimore).

"Status of Women Microbiologists," *Science*, 1974 (with Eva Ruth Kashket et al.).

Pollard, Morris., ed. "Defective Interfering Particles as Antiviral Agents" in *Perspectives in Virology*, 1975 (with Eduardo L. Palma).

Fraenkel-Conrat, H. and R. R. Wagner, eds. "Defective Interfering Animal Viruses," *Comprehensive Virology*, 1977 (with Baltimore).

Moon, (R. L. and D. D. Whitt, eds. "Virology," *Highlights in Microbiology*, 1981.

Domingo, Estaban, John J. Holland, and Paul Ahlquist., eds. "Modulation of Viral Diseases by Defective Interfering Particles," *RNA Genetics: 3, Variability of RNA Genomes*, 1988.

"Science Education Shouldn't Be Restricted to Narrow Boxes," *Scientist*, 1992.

"How Does Variation Count?," *Nature*, 1992 (with John M. Coffin).

About Huang

Miller, Susan Katz. "Asian-Americans Bump Against Glass Ceilings." *Science* 258 (November 13, 1992).

McMurray, Emily J., ed. *Notable Twentieth-Century Scientists*. Detroit, Mich.: Gale Research, 1995.

Who's Who in America. New Providence, N.J.: Marquis Who's Who, 1995.

(Rose Secrest)

Ruth Hubbard

Disciplines: Biology, chemistry, and genetics

Contribution: A biochemist who studied chemicals involved in vision, Hubbard became a leading scientific critic of genetic research on gender-role differences and other human traits.

Mar. 3, 1924	Born in Vienna, Austria
1938	Leaves Austria with her family after the Nazi invasion
1942	Works in George Wald's laboratory at Harvard University
1946	Begins graduate studies at Radcliffe College, Harvard
1948	Receives a fellowship to study at University College Medical School, London
1950	Earns a Ph.D. in biology from Harvard
1952-53	Works at the Carlsberg Laboratory, in Copenhagen, Denmark, on a Guggenheim Fellowship
1954	Takes a position as a research fellow in Wald's laboratory
1958	Promoted to research associate
1958	Marries George Wald
1974	Becomes the first woman to receive tenure at Harvard in the natural sciences
1979	Edits *Women Look at Biology Looking at Women* and *Genes and Gender 2*
1990	Retires as professor emerita
1993	Publishes *Exploding the Gene Myth*

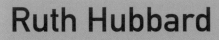

Early Life

Ruth Hubbard was born Ruth Hoffman in 1924. Her parents, Richard and Helene (Ehrlich) Hoffman, were physicians. They settled in Boston after fleeing Nazi persecution in Austria.

Ruth entered Radcliffe College, Harvard, expecting to continue the family medical tradition. In her native country, women of her class usually entered a profession and left childcare to servants.

Hoffman did not seriously consider a scientific career, even though she enjoyed science classes, because subtle messages constantly signaled that research science was not for women. During her senior year, however, she worked in the laboratory of George Wald, who was working on infrared vision. This experience turned her away from medicine and toward laboratory science.

Hoffman married Frank Twombly Hubbard on December 26, 1942. He was in the Army, and she moved to Chattanooga, Tennessee, where he was stationed, in 1945. Wanting to help in the war against the Nazis, Hubbard worked as a laboratory technician for the Tennessee Public Health Service. The marriage ended in divorce in 1951.

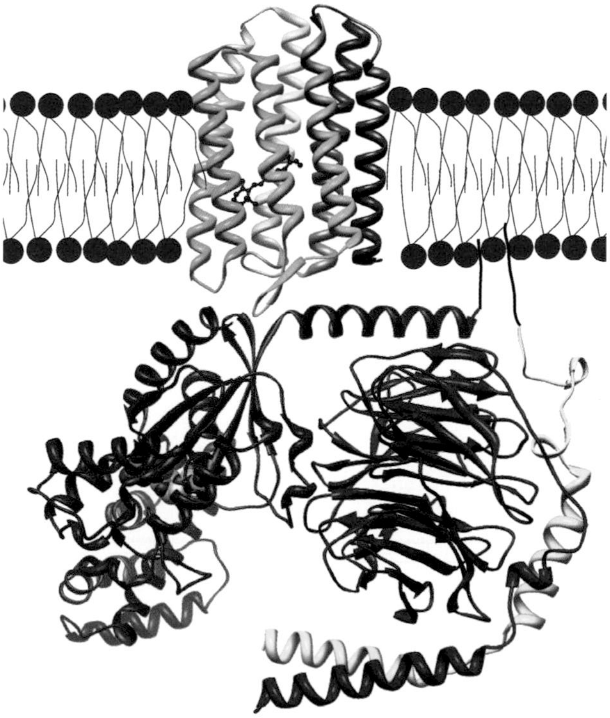

When studying vision, Hubbard investigated the chemical structure of rhodopsin.

A Female Scientist at Harvard

Hubbard returned to Radcliffe in 1946 to begin a Ph.D. program in biology, resuming work in Wald's laboratory. After receiving her doctorate, she stayed on at Harvard for another forty years.

Like most women in science during the 1950s and 1960s, Hubbard held appointments that offered no prospects of a tenured faculty position. She was a research fellow from 1950 to 1952 and from 1954 to 1958, and later served as a research associate and lecturer, from 1958 to 1974. Hubbard and George Wald were married on June 11, 1958.

Hubbard studied the biochemistry of vision, experimenting on frogs, cattle, and squid. She investigated the chemical structure of rhodopsin, which responds to light, and other pigments found in the eye.

She and her coworkers found that among the different forms of vitamin A, which is involved in vision, only one helps produce rhodopsin. They also found that light changes the shape of certain visual pigments, leading to the creation of electrical charges involved in nerve transmission.

Studying Science and Society

During the Vietnam War, Hubbard began questioning the role of laboratory science. She began to wonder why scientists do what they do. She asked herself whether it was worth killing squid, which she found beautiful, for the sake of research.

Hubbard became interested in the politics of women's healthcare. The growing women's movement in the early 1970s led her to rethink her own career. She joined a group investigating the status of women at Harvard, where the only woman then holding a full professorship occupied a chair endowed specifically for a female.

After 1980 Hubbard's research focused on the history and sociology of medical genetics and human behavioral genetics. She wrote and lectured on the ways in which social ideas have influenced scientists' work, on the impact of science on society, and on the need for nonscientists to participate in public debates on science.

Bibliography

By Hubbard

Genes and Gender 2: Pitfalls in Research on Sex and Gender, 1979 (as editor, with Marian Lowe).

Women Look at Biology Looking at Women: A Collection of Feminist Critiques, 1979 (as editor, with Mary Sue Henifin and Barbara Fried).

Woman's Nature: Rationalizations of Inequality, 1983 (as editor).

The Shape of Red: Insider/Outsider Reflections, 1988 (as editor, with Margaret Randall).

The Politics of Women's Biology, 1990.

Exploding the Gene Myth: How Genetic Information Is Produced and Manipulated by Scientists, Physicians, Employers, Insurance Companies, Educators, and Law Enforcers, 1993 (with Elijah Wald).

About Hubbard

Holloway, Marguerite "Turning the Inside Out." *Scientific American* 272 (June, 1995).

Davidson, M. "'You've Got a Long Way to Go, Baby': A Conversation About the Women's Movement with Ruth Hubbard." *USA Today* 116 (September, 1987).

(Bonnie Ellen Blustein)

Scientific and Social Ideas Are Intertwined

A scientific study of society requires an understanding of how social prejudices such as sexism and racism have been incorporated into biology, especially through genetic determinism.

Genetic determinism is an ideology that often guides biological research and sociological theorizing. It claims that individual traits (both social and medical) are inherited and can best be studied at the molecular level. Genetic determinism also claims that social institutions and public health trends can best be studied by investigating individual traits. Some argue, however, that genetic determinism is not scientifically valid.

Hubbard claimed that categories such as "race" and "sex" single out certain biological traits and use them to separate people who have far more biological traits in common. She sees them as social categories, not simple biological facts. She felt that scientists should take this into account when designing research projects, or they run the risk of recycling stereotypes instead of advancing scientific knowledge.

Genes and environments interact in very complex ways. The same gene expresses itself differently in different environments. Even within the same environment, organisms with identical genes often develop differently. Genetic determinism therefore limits the ability of medical science to understand and treat illnesses such as heart disease and cancer.

Bibliography

Sayers, Janet. *Biological Politics: Feminist and Anti-Feminist Perspectives*. London: Tavistock, 1982.

Weir, Robert F., Susan C. Lawrence, and Evan Fales., eds. *Genes and Human Self-Knowledge: Historical and Philosophical Reflections on Modern Genetics*. Iowa City: University of Iowa Press, 1994.

Lewontin, R. C., Steven Rose, and Leon J. Kamin. *Not in Our Genes: Biology, Ideology, and Human Nature*. New York: Pantheon Books, 1984.

Wilhelm Ludvig Johannsen

Disciplines: Biology, botany, genetics, and physiology

Contribution: Johannsen helped establish the field of genetics with his experimental support for and invention of the terms "gene," "genotype," and "phenotype."

Feb. 3, 1857	Born in Copenhagen, Denmark
1881	Appointed an assistant chemist at Carlsberg Laboratorium, Copenhagen
1892	Becomes a lecturer at the Royal Veterinary and Agricultural College, Copenhagen
1893	Demonstrates his technique of using ether to break the dormancy of plants
1893-1897	Carries out individual progeny analyses of barley and the common bean
1898	Elected to the Royal Danish Academy of Sciences
1902-1909	Conducts pure line studies of the common bean
1905	Appointed *professor honoris* at the University of Copenhagen
1909	Coins the terms "gene," "genotype," and "phenotype"
1910	Named *doctor honoris causa* in medicine at the University of Copenhagen
1917	Becomes rector of the University of Copenhagen
1924	Elected president of the International Seed Control Congress
Nov. 11, 1927	Dies in Copenhagen

Early Life

Wilhelm Ludvig Johannsen (pronounced "yoh-HAN-suhn") was born in 1857. The son of a Danish army officer, he credited both of his parents for helping him to become a scientist. His punctual, orderly father gave him an interest in the material aspects of things, and his mother's love of plants and animals led to his fascination with nature.

Johannsen passed his qualifying examinations for the university at the age of fifteen, but his parents could only afford to send his elder brother. Instead, Wilhelm was apprenticed to a pharmacist in 1872, passed his examination in 1879 with high honors, and continued his studies in botany and chemistry until he was appointed to the chemical department at Carlsberg Laboratorium in Copenhagen in 1881.

Johannsen gained initial fame and election to the Danish Academy of Sciences with his discovery that ether could be used to "awaken" plants from their winter dormancy.

He also traveled to gain additional experience in plant physiology, and, by 1892 he was a lecturer in botany and plant physiology at the Royal Veterinary and Agricultural College in Copenhagen.

The Experimental Years

Johannsen began studying why the characteristics of self-fertilized plants such as barley (*Hordeum vulgare*) and the common bean (*Phaseolus vulgaris*) vary. He found that the average weight of seeds from parents and offspring were the same, even when he had selected for heavier or lighter seeds. He introduced his concept of "pure lines" in 1903, the same year that he was promoted to professor.

Later that year, Johannsen read about the stability of inherited traits as demonstrated by Gregor Mendel and integrated these ideas into his theory of evolution. His textbook on heredity, *Arvelighedslaerens elementer*, was published in 1905. That same year, Johannsen was hired at the University of Copenhagen, a move of which some peers disapproved because he lacked a university education. His increasing fame stifled the criticism.

Writer, Critic, and Historian

Johannsen expanded his textbook in German, and it was published in 1909 entitled *Elemente der exakten Erblichkeitslehre.* In it, he introduced statistical methodology and the terms "gene," "genotype," and "phenotype." The book became the most influential genetics text in Europe.

Genotype Versus Phenotype

The external appearance of an individual organism (phenotype) is distinguished from the genetic material inherited from its parents (genotype).

Johannsen was the first to divide variation into two components. He studied "pure lines," or all individual plants descended from a single self-fertilized individual, in order to determine whether offspring selected for smaller or larger seed weights would vary significantly from parents. He found no difference between the averages of the parental line and the averages of selected subpopulations of offspring.

Johannsen concluded that change could only result from inherited differences in pure lines. The differences among pure lines, the genotype, included all the genes in the fertilized egg. (He coined the term "gene" but refused to identify it physically.)

He recognized that the genotype interacted with the environment to produce external characteristics, but his first definition of phenotype referred to the population average of the distribution of variation. By the 1926 edition of his book *Elemente der exakten Erblichkeitslehre*, Johannsen had been influenced by Thomas Hunt Morgan's group working on the genetics of the fruit fly (*Drosophila melanogaster*), and he also applied his phenotype concept to the external traits of individual organisms, the contemporary meaning of the term.

The relationship between genotype and phenotype, and how phenotype is expressed and why it varies (phenotypic plasticity), are areas of ongoing research.

Bibliography

Lewin, *V.* Benjamin. *Genes.* Oxford, England: Oxford University Press, 1993.

West-Eberhard, Mary Jane. "Phenotypic Plasticity and the Origins of Diversity." *Annual Review of Ecology and Systematics* 20 (1989).

Dawkins, Richard. *The Selfish Gene.* 2d ed. Oxford, England: Oxford University Press, 1989.

By 1910, Johannsen was named doc*tor honoris causa* in medicine. He no longer experimented but instead interpreted and synthesized current thought.

He wrote a paper in 1914 entitled *Falske analogier*, in which he criticized the use of speculation and mysticism in biology. He also explored the history of genetics in the popular book named *Arvelighed i historisk og experimentel belysning* (1917).

Resting on His Laurels

Johannsen became rector of the University of Copenhagen in 1917 and received many additional academic honors from outside Denmark. He had originally regretted his lack of university training, but, in retrospect, he felt that it contributed to his originality. He used his gifts, including a superb memory, fluency, and wit, to make difficult concepts accessible to a broader audience.

Johannsen died in 1927 in Copenhagen at the age of seventy.

Bibliography

By Johannsen

Laerebog i plantefisiologi med henblik paa plantedyrkningen, 1892 (textbook on plant physiology with special reference to plant cultivation).

Om arvelighed og variabilitet, 1896 (on heredity and variation).

Das Aether-Verfahren beim Frühtreiben mit besonderer Berücksichtigung der Fliedertreiberei, 1900 (the ether process).

Über Erblichkeit in Populationen und in reinen Linien, Ein Beitrag zur Beleuchtung schwebender Selektionsfragen, 1903 ("Concerning Heredity in Populations and in Pure Lines" in *Selected Readings in Biology for Natural Sciences* 3, 1955).

Arvelighedslaerens elementer: Forelasninger holdte ved Kobenhavns universitet, 1905 (elements of heredity).

Elemente der exakten Erblichkeitslehre, 1909 (elements of an exact science of heredity).

Falske analogier, med henblik paa lighed, slaegtskab, arv, tradition og udvikling, 1914 (false analogies).

Arvelighed i historisk og experimentel belysning, 1917 (heredity in the light of history and experimental study).

About Johannsen

Dunn, Leslie Clarence. "Johannsen, Wilhelm Ludwig." in *Dictionary of Scientific Biography*, edited by Charles Coulston Gillispie. Vol. 7. New York: Charles Scribner's Sons, 1970.

Bowler, Peter J. *The Mendelian Revolution*. Baltimore, Md.: The Johns Hopkins University Press, 1989.

Bowler, Peter J. *The Origins of Theoretical Population Genetics*. Chicago, Ill.: University of Chicago Press, 1971.

(Joan C. Stevenson)

Helen Dean King

Disciplines: Cell biology and genetics

Contribution: King produced standard strains of laboratory rats used worldwide for experimental studies.

Sept. 27, 1869	Born in Owego, New York
1892	Earns an A.B. from Vassar College, New York
1899	Earns an A.M. and a Ph.D. from Bryn Mawr College, Pennsylvania
1899-1904	Hired as a biology assistant at Bryn Mawr
1899-1907	Teaches science at Miss Florence Baldwin's School in Bryn Mawr
1906	Designated among the top 1,000 U.S. scientists in the first edition of *American Men of Science*
1906-1908	Named a biology research fellow at the University of Pennsylvania
1908-1913	Serves as an anatomy assistant at the Wistar Institute of Anatomy and Biology
1913-1927	Named assistant anatomy professor at the Wistar Institute
1919	Publishes *Studies on Inbreeding*
1924-1927	Edits *Journal of Morphology and Physiology*
1927-1949	Named an embryology professor at the Wistar Institute
1932	Shares the Ellen Richards Prize
1939	Publishes *Life Processes in Gray Norway Rats During Fourteen Years in Captivity*
Mar. 7, 1955	Dies in Philadelphia, Pennsylvania

Early Life

Helen Dean King, the daughter of George Alonzo and Leonora Louise Dean King, grew up in a prosperous family. After graduating from the Owego Free Academy, King enrolled at Vassar College in 1888. Vassar supported scientific study for women, purchasing new equipment and hiring talented professors who were familiar with current theories and techniques.

King completed her degree in 1892 and worked in the biology laboratory. By 1895, she began a doctorate at Bryn Mawr College. She focused on morphology, studying with the noted geneticist Thomas Hunt Morgan, who encouraged women to pursue independent research projects.

King worked as Morgan's assistant for five years after her graduation in 1899. She published her doctoral dissertation about embryonic development of toads in 1901. During this time, she also taught science in a local school.

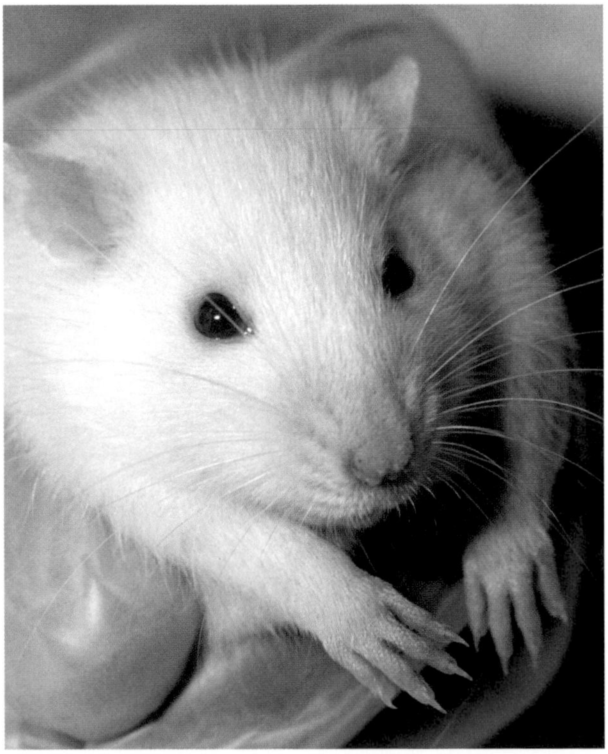

Rats are crucial for laboratory studies, and King developed standard strains to aid experiments.

Research with Inbreeding

By 1906, King was employed as a biological research fellow at the University of Pennsylvania. Interested in fertilization, she examined factors such as environmental, genetic, and chemical influences on gender determination.

In 1908, she was named an assistant at the Wistar Institute of Anatomy and Biology, where King's most significant work occurred.

She began her albino rat-breeding experiments in 1909. She bred two males and two females from the same litter. King then carefully selected their offspring, ultimately producing twenty-five succeeding generations.

The King colony established a uniform stock of white rats that were used in research laboratories worldwide. The rats were large, fertile, and lived for a long time. King admitted that she could not solely credit inbreeding with these improved traits but emphasized that inbreeding had not caused the damage that Charles Darwin had hypothesized.

Animal Research

King developed standard strains of rats used in research laboratories. The use of animals in experimentation, however, has been a controversial topic.

Animal research is the use of animals in experiments to test surgical techniques, drug effects, and disease treatments. Scientists and animal rights activists have debated the use of animals in scientific and medical investigations.

Throughout history, humans have utilized animals for scientific pursuits. Early scientists dissected animals to understand anatomy. Since the nineteenth century, animals have been used to produce vaccines against diseases. Louis Pasteur developed protective animal cultures to combat cholera and anthrax.

Animal research advocates stress biomedical gains, including the vaccine to fight Hemophilus influenza type B (Hib), which causes meningitis. Laboratory animals have enabled researchers to extract insulin, produce antibiotics and antibacterial agents, perfect organ transplants, and practice heart surgery.

The animal rights movement emerged in the 1970s, demanding humane treatment of laboratory animals. Its leaders argue that animal research cannot consistently be applied to humans and that laboratory results are often misleading.

These critics claim that specimens, under stress in laboratory conditions, produce antibodies and hormones that skew tests. They argue that drugs deemed nontoxic in animals have caused severe reactions, even fatalities, in humans.

Urging scientists to embrace alternatives, animal rights activists suggest that researchers observe humans and consider factors such as genetic, environmental, and biochemical causes of diseases. The ethical and moral aspects of animal research present a complex issue that is not readily resolved.

Bibliography

Rowan, Andrew N., Franklin M. Loew, and Joan C. Weer. *The Animal Research Controversy: Protest, Process, and Public Policy*. Medford, Mass.: Center for Animals and Public Policy, Tufts University School of Veterinary Medicine, 1995.

Rowan, Andrew N. "Forum: The Benefits and Ethics of Animal Research." *Scientific American* 276, no. 2 (February, 1997).

Orlans, F. Barbara. *In the Name of Science: Issues in Responsible Animal Experimentation*. New York: Oxford University Press, 1993.

Blum, Deborah. *The Monkey Wars*. New York: Oxford University Press, 1994.

Negative Publicity and Further Studies

Many U.S. newspapers portrayed King as an immoral woman for her genetic research. Reporters questioned her femininity because she handled rats and hinted that she believed human inbreeding would strengthen society. Outraged readers sent her angry letters, including death threats. King ignored public opinion, however, and continued to teach and to conduct research. She served on the Wistar Institute's advisory board and was editor of its bibliographic service.

In 1919, King pursued new inbreeding studies with rats. She domesticated the wild Norway rats that roamed Philadelphia's streets. She successfully bred six pairs of the Norway rats through twenty-eight generations.

King noticed slight mutations in the animals. Some were hairless, while others had wavy hair. New fur colors were seen, and a "waltzing rat" ran around in circles. She concluded that captivity encouraged diversity, not similarity. King bred rats for scientists wishing to examine specific characteristics or problems.

Honors

King's rat-breeding experiments earned scientific accolades. She was elected vice president of the American Society of Zoologists in 1937 and was named a Fellow of the New York Academy of Science. Her entry was starred in the first edition of *American Men of Science* (and following editions), indicating her status as being among the top 1,000 U.S. scientists and attesting her peers' respect for her research.

King was honored with the Ellen Richards Prize for outstanding experimental work conducted by a female scientist. Her successes inspired breeders of racehorses and sporting animals to improve their livestock through inbreeding. Her rats enabled scientific investigations and medical advances that have benefitted humanity. King died in 1955.

Bibliography

By King

"The Maturation and Fertilization of the Egg of *Bufo lentiginosus*," *Journal of Morphology*, 1901.

"The Growth and Variability in the Body Weight of the Albino Rat," *Anatomical Record*, 1915.

"The Relation of Age to Fertility in the Rat," *Anatomical Record*, 1916.

"Ruby-Eyed Dilute Gray, a Third Allelomorph in the Albino Series of the Rat," *Journal of Experimental Zoology*, 1918 (with P. W. Whiting).

"Studies on Inbreeding: I. The Effects of Inbreeding on the Growth and Variability in the Body Weight of the Albino Rat," *Journal of Experimental Zoology*, 1918.

"Studies on Inbreeding: II. The Effects of Inbreeding on the Fertility and on the Constitutional Vigor of the Albino Rat," *Journal of Experimental Zoology*, 1918.

"Studies on Inbreeding: III. The Effects of Inbreeding, with Selection, on the Sex Ratio of the Albino Rat," *Journal of Experimental Zoology*, 1918.

"Studies on Inbreeding: IV A Further Study of the Effects of Inbreeding on the Growth and Variability in the Body Weight of the Albino Rat," *Journal of Experimental Zoology*, 1919.

Studies on Inbreeding, 1919.

Life Processes in Gray Norway Rats During Fourteen Years in Captivity, 1939.

About King

"Dr. Helen King, 85, Noted Zoologist." *New York Times* 104 (March 10, 1955).

Lindell, Ann. "Helen Dean King." *in Notable Women in the Life Sciences*, edited by Benjamin F. and Barbara Smith Shearer. Westport, Conn.: Greenwood Press, 1996.

Bogin, Mary. "Helen Dean King." In *Dictionary of Scientific Biography*. Vol. 17, suppl. 2. New York: Charles Scribner's Sons, 1990.

(Elizabeth D. Schafer)

Arthur Kornberg

Disciplines: Biology, genetics, and medicine
Contribution: Kornberg was awarded the 1959 Nobel Prize in Physiology or Medicine for his isolation of deoxyribonucleic acid (DNA) polymerase, the enzyme in bacteria that catalyzes the replication of genetic material.

Mar. 3, 1918	Born in Brooklyn, New York
1941	Graduates with an M.D. from University of Rochester School of Medicine
1942	Enlists in the U.S. Coast Guard
1942-1945	Transferred to the nutrition section of the National Institute of Health (NIH)
1946	Studies enzymatic techniques at New York University
1947	Trains with Carl and Gerty Cori at the Washington University School of Medicine in St. Louis
1947-1952	Returns to NIH as chief of the enzyme and metabolism section
1953-1959	Serves as professor and chair of the microbiology department at the Washington University School of Medicine
1959-1969	Serves as professor and chair of the biochemistry department at the Stanford University School of Medicine
1959	Awarded the Nobel Prize in Physiology or Medicine
1967	Publishes work on the enzymatic synthesis of DNA
1970	Elected a member of the Royal Society of London

Early Life

Arthur Kornberg was born on March 3, 1918 to Jewish parents Joseph and Lena (née Katz) Kornberg. His father was a sewing machine operator in the sweatshops of the Lower East Side of New York City. A brilliant student who skipped several grades, Arthur graduated from Abraham Lincoln High School at the age of fifteen and enrolled in a premedical program at the City College of New York.

Receiving his B.S. degree in 1937, Kornberg entered the medical school at the University of Rochester. While a student, Kornberg became aware of a mild jaundice (yellowing) in his eyes. He observed a similar condition among other students and patients at the hospital and published these findings in his first professional paper in the *Journal of Clinical Investigation*.

Following his graduation in 1941, Kornberg enlisted in the U.S. Coast Guard, being assigned duty as a medical officer in the Caribbean.

Officials at the National Institute of Health (NIH), aware of his brief excursion into the subject of jaundice, arranged for Kornberg's transfer to the institute. He spent the remainder of World War II years carrying out research in the nutrition laboratory there.

In 1943, Kornberg married Sylvy Levy. In addition to being the mother of three children, Sylvy was a researcher herself. Her suggestions and advice would play important roles in Kornberg's research.

Enzyme Research

Bored with nutrition studies, Kornberg decided on a leave of absence to study enzyme function. He spent a year with Severo Ochoa at the New York University School of Medicine and a year with Carl and Gerty Cori at the Washington University School of Medicine.

During the summer of 1953, Kornberg enrolled in a microbiology course offered by Cornelius van Niel in Pacific Grove, California. Kornberg had recently accepted a position as chair of the department of biochemistry at the Washington University School of Medicine in St. Louis, and he felt the need for more formal instruction in the subject.

In addition to receiving a historical overview of the subject, Kornberg became intrigued with bacteria as a source of enzymes for his research. In particular, he became interested in biosynthetic pathways for the building blocks of deoxyribonucleic acid (DNA). Once he was able to work out their synthesis, it was a logical step to search for the enzyme that assembled them into DNA itself.

The Isolation of DNA Polymerase

Using extracts from the bacterium Escherichia coli, *Kornberg and his coworkers were able to purify the enzyme that replicates deoxyribonucleic acid (DNA), called DNA polymerase.*

Kornberg did not initially set out with the intention of isolating the replicative enzyme for DNA. His work at the Washington University School of Medicine during this period dealt with the question of the pathway for synthesis of nucleotide bases found in ribonucleic acid (RNA) and DNA. Much of the research during 1953 and 1954 dealt with purification of the enzymes that synthesize the precursors of DNA. By 1954, Kornberg's team had firmly established how the nucleotides are synthesized. The next logical step was to study how they are assembled into DNA or RNA.

Initial experiments with extracts from animal cells were unsuccessful, and Kornberg turned to extracts from the bacterium *Escherichia coli* (*E. coli*). In November, 1955, Kornberg and coworkers Robert Lehman and Maurice Bessman began the purification of the DNA replicative enzyme.

Kornberg determined that preformed DNA had to be present in the assay mixture. By June, 1956, he was able to report they had isolated a fraction from *E. coli* that could synthesize DNA.

The next months consisted of further isolations. By the summer of 1957, Kornberg had completed the purification, demonstrating that the enzyme was capable of synthesizing DNA. Ironically, the papers that were submitted with reports of the findings were initially rejected.

Bibliography

Kornberg, Arthur and Tania Baker. *DNA Replication.* 2d ed. New York: W. H. Freeman, 1992.

Darnell, James et al. *Molecular Cell Biology.* New York: W. H. Freeman, 1990.

Hanawalt, Philip C. *Molecules to Living Cells.* San Francisco, Calif.: W. H. Freeman, 1980.

By 1957, Kornberg was able to report the isolation of the DNA-synthesizing enzyme, which he called DNA polymerase. In recognition of his work, Kornberg was awarded the 1959 Nobel Prize in Physiology or Medicine. In 1967, Mehran Goulian and Kornberg reported that their enzyme was able to synthesize biologically active DNA in a test tube.

Recognition

The Nobel Prize was one of many awards for Kornberg. Among other aspects of national and international recognition were the Paul-Lewis Award from the American Chemical Society in 1951, the Scientific Achievement Award from the American Medical Association in 1968, and the National Medal of Science in 1980. In addition, Kornberg was elected as a foreign member of the Royal Society of London.

Bibliography

By Kornberg

"Latent Liver Disease in Persons Recovered from Catarrhal Jaundice and in Otherwise Normal Medical Students as Revealed by Bilirubin Excretion Test," *Journal of Clinical Investigation*, 1942.

"Mechanism of Production of Vitamin K Deficiency in Rats by Sulfonamides," *Journal of Biological Chemistry*, 1944.

"Enzymatic Synthesis of Deoxyribonucleic Acid: I. Preparation of Substrates and Partial Purification of an Enzyme from *Escherichia coli*," *Journal of Biological Chemistry*, 1958.

"Biologic Synthesis of Deoxyribonucleic Acid," *Science*, 1960.

Enzymatic Synthesis of DNA, 1961.

"Enzymatic Synthesis of DNA: XXIII. Synthesis of Circular Replicative Form of Phage ΦX174 DNA," *Proceedings of the National Academy of Sciences*, 1967 (with Mehran Goulian).

"Enzymatic Synthesis of DNA: XXIV. Synthesis of Infectious Phage ΦX174 DNA," *Proceedings of the National Academy of Sciences*, 1967 (with Goulian and R. Sinsheimer).

DNA Synthesis, 1974.

DNA Replication, 1980 (2d ed., 1992, with Tania Baker).

"Initiation of Enzymatic Replication at the Origin of the *Escherichia coli* Chromosome," *Proceedings of the National Academy of Sciences*, 1985 (with T. Ogawa et al.).

"DNA Replication," *Journal of Biological Chemistry*, 1988.

For the Love of Enzymes: The Odyssey of a Bio-chemist, 1989.

The Golden Helix: Inside Biotech Ventures, 1995.

About Kornberg

Magill, Frank N., ed. "Arthur Kornberg." in The Nobel Prize Winners: Physiology or Medicine. Pasadena, Calif.: Salem Press, 1991.

Tyler Wasson, ed. *Nobel Prize Winners*. Bronx, N.Y.: H. W. Wilson, 1987.

McMurray, Emily J., ed. *Notable Twentieth-Century Scientists*. Detroit, Mich.: Gale Research, 1995.

(Richard Adler)

Albrecht Kossel

Disciplines: Chemistry and physiology

Contribution: A pioneer in the chemistry of nucleic acids, Kossel isolated and established the composition of these cell constituents.

Sept. 16, 1853	Born in Rostock, Mecklenburg (now Germany)
1878	Earns an M.D. from the University of Strasbourg
1883	Named chemical director of the Institute of Physiology in Berlin
1884	Identifies histone proteins in the nucleus
1885	Discovers adenine and guanine in nucleic acids
1891	Identifies the presence of a carbohydrate in nucleic acids
1894	Discovers cytosine and thymine in nucleic acids
1895	Becomes a professor of physiology at Marburg University
1895	Named editor of the *Zeitschrift für physiologische Chemie*
1896	Discovers the amino acid histidine
1901	Becomes director of the Institute of Physiology at the University of Heidelberg
1910	Awarded the Nobel Prize in Physiology or Medicine
1912	Proposes that nuclear proteins are the chemical basis for biological specificity
July 5, 1927	Dies in Heidelberg, Germany

Early Life

Karl Martin Leonhard Albrecht Kossel (pronounced "KOHS-uhl") developed an interest in botany as a teenager, becoming an expert on the flora of the Rostock region of Germany. His father, a merchant, discouraged this interest, seeing no future economic value in it. In 1872, Kossel entered the University of Strasbourg as a medical student. He received an M.D. in 1878 but never practiced medicine. He remained at Strasbourg until 1883 as a research scientist in the field of biochemistry.

From 1883 to 1895, he was the chemical director of the Institute of Physiology in Berlin. In 1886, he married Luise Holtzmann and their son, Walther, became an eminent theoretical physicist.

Research in Strasbourg and Berlin

Kossel's first publications appeared in 1878. In 1879, he began to study substances of unknown nature in the cell nucleus. He made these his life's work.

Kossel developed the first reliable methods to isolate and analyze nuclear substances. He separated them into protein, nonprotein, and phosphoric acid components. In 1885, he discovered that the nonprotein part contained adenine and guanine. These were purines (nitrogen-containing heterocyclic organic bases). By 1894, Koseel had found two additional bases: cytosine and thymine. These were pyrimidines, another group of heterocyclic substances.

By 1894, he had discovered yet another component of nucleic acids. There was a carbohydrate entity present, but he was never able to determine its nature.

The Marburg Years

Kossel's position at the Institute of Physiology was financially unattractive, and his heavy administrative duties limited his research activity. In 1895, he became a professor of physiology at the University of Marburg. There he was able to develop his research plans and attract an international group of graduate and postdoctoral students.

At Marburg, he became increasingly interested in the proteins of the cell nucleus. He recognized that the nucleic acids are always associated with them and named this new class of conjugated proteins "nucleoproteins."

Many nuclear proteins had a basic and relatively simple nature, and these he named "histones." In 1896 their hydrolysis yielded several basic amino acids, including a hitherto unknown one: histidine. He believed histones to be the core building blocks of the complex proteins of the body.

From 1895, Kossel was editor of the *Zeitschrift fiir physiologische Chemie*, the first journal devoted to the subject later named biochemistry.

The Role of Nucleic Acids in the Cell

Kossel's findings on nucleic acids were the foundation for the discovery of their biological function.

Kossel obtained all the chemical components of nucleic acids, but much remained unclear. No one knew how the organic bases, carbohydrate, and phosphoric acid were linked in nucleic acids or what the nature of the carbohydrate was. His successors solved these problems by the 1940s, disclosing that nucleic acids had one of two carbohydrates. Some had D-ribose; some had deoxy-D-ribose. This discovery became the basis for classifying nucleic acids into ribonucleic acid (RNA) and deoxyribonucleic acid (DNA) types.

Kossel speculated about the biological role of nucleic acids. He proposed that they were essential for the growth of tissues. He knew that nucleoproteins are found in the chromosomes of germ cells and thus are transmitted to new cells. He believed, however, that nucleic acids were too simple and that only the proteins had sufficient diversity to function in the transmission of hereditary characteristics.

Kossel's findings took on new meaning as scientists in the 1950s discovered that DNA produces genetic effects and that RNA conveys genetic information to cells. These discoveries put Kossel's work into the context of a new molecular genetics. DNA became the storage molecule of genetic information, RNA the molecule of gene expression, and Kossel's histone the molecule of gene suppression.

Bibliography

Stein, Gary, Janet Stein, and Lewis Kleinsmith. "Chromosomal Proteins and Gene Regulation." *Scientific American* 232 (February, 1975).

Levene, P. A. and Lawrence Bass *Nucleic Acids*. New York: Chemical Catalog Company, 1931.

Olby, Robert. *The Path to the Double Helix*. Seattle, Wash.: University of Washington Press, 1974.

Heidelberg and World War I

From 1901 until his retirement in 1924, Kossel was director of the physiological institute at Heidelberg University, Germany. In 1910, he received the Nobel Prize in Physiology or Medicine for his studies on the chemistry of cell constituents. His fortunes faded from 1914. He was ostracized by his fellow German academics because he opposed World War I and refused to sign the 1914 pronouncement of German professors justifying the war. Kossel never regained the influence that he once had. He died in 1927.

Bibliography

By Kossel

Untersuchungen über die Nukleine und ihre Spaltungsprodukte, 1881 (investigations into the nucleins and their cleavage products).

Zur Chemie die Zellkernig, 1882 (chemistry of the cell nucleus).

Leitfaden für medizinisch-chemische Kurse, 1888 (textbook for medical-chemical courses).

Die Gewebe des menschlichen Körpers und ihre mikroskopische Untersuchung, 1889-1891 (with Paul Schiefferdecker and Wilhelm Julius Behrens; the tissues in the human body and their microscopic invsestigation).

von Meyer, E., ed."Beziehungen der Chemie zur Physiologie" (the relationship between chemistry and physiology) in *Die Kultur der Gegenwart ihre Entwicklung und ihre Ziele: Chemie*, 1913.

The Protamines and Histones, 1928.

The Chemical Composition of the Cell, 1911-1912.

About Kossel

Farber, Eduard., ed. "Albrecht Kossel." in *Great Chemists*. New York: Interscience, 1961.

Fruton, Joseph S. *Molecules and Life*. New York: Interscience, 1972.

Kennaway, Ernest. "Some Recollections of Albrecht Kossel." *Annals of Science* 8 (1952).

(Albert B. Costa)

Eric S. Lander

Areas of Achievement: Mathematics, molecular biology, medicine, and genomics.

Contribution: Lander led the Human Genome Project and pioneered the application of genomics to the understanding of human disease. He is the founder of the Broad Institute.

Feb. 3, 1957	Born in Brooklyn, New York
1978	Earned a B.A. in mathematics from Princeton University
1981	Awarded Ph.D. in mathematics, University of Oxford
1981-1990	Assistant and associate professor of managerial economics at Harvard
1986	Joined Whitehead Institute for Biomedical Research at Massachusetts Institute of Technology
1987	Awarded MacArthur Fellowship's "genius" grant
1990	Founded the WICGR (Whitehead Institute/MIT Center for Genome Research)
1997	Elected a member of the U.S. National Academy of Sciences
1999	Elected to the US Institute of Medicine
2003	Completed mapping the human blueprint as a principal leader of the international Human Genome Project
2008	Co-chair of President Obama's Council of Advisors on Science and Technology
2012	Received the Dan David Prize
2013	Awarded the $3 million Breakthrough Prize in Life Sciences

Early Life

Eric Steven Lander grew up in Flatlands, a working-class neighborhood in Brooklyn, New York. His father, a lawyer, died of multiple sclerosis, when Lander was only 11 years old. His mother, though also lawyer, encountered much sexism in the field and had to turn to teaching to support Lander and his brother. Lander attended Stuyvesant High School in Manhattan, an elite public school specializing in mathematics and science. He led the math team.

At age 17, a paper Lander wrote on quasi perfect numbers won the national Westinghouse Science Talent Search. He attended the Academy of Achievement's 1974 program in Salt Lake City as a student delegate. He was also selected to participate on the U.S. team in the 1974 International Mathematical Olympiad, a competition begun in 1959 for high school students. It was the first time the United States had sent a team to the contest—the team placed second behind the Soviet Union.

Lander attended Princeton University, where he majored in mathematics. He graduated valedictorian at the age of 20, and was awarded the Pyne Prize, the university's highest undergraduate honor. With a Rhodes scholarship, Lander continued his studies at the University of Oxford in England, where, in only two years, he earned a Ph.D. in mathematics in 1981.

From Math to Genetics

It looked as if Lander would base his career in mathematics, but after Oxford, he returned to the United States to teach managerial economics—a subject he had never studied—at the Harvard Business School. He said he taught himself as he went along. However, managerial economics did not seem to fulfill him.

After consulting with his brother, Arthur, a neurobiologist, Lander developed an interest in biology and, ultimately, genetics. He frequented a fruit-fly genetics lab at Harvard, sat in on undergraduate lab classes and moonlighted in the molecular genetic laboratory. A few years later, he was pursuing genetics research at the Massachusetts Institute of Technology (MIT), where his mathematics background proved invaluable in identifying the minute genetic variations that predispose individuals to a host of disorders, including cancer, diabetes, schizophrenia, and obesity.

Broad Institute of MIT and Harvard

Lander has been at the forefront of encouraging and fostering scientific collaboration. In 2003, Lander helped found the Broad Institute of MIT and Harvard, a biomedical research organization specializing in genomic medicine. The institute is a joint effort between Harvard and MIT that supports the collaboration of nearly 2,000 scientists in biology, genetics, and genomics. Lander's idea was to encourage scientists to work together to transform medicine.

He hopes that the Institute will reveal the fundamental mechanisms of diseases and develop new ways to create medicines to treat them. The Institute has several goals, Lander says, that will "transform the process of therapeutic discovery and development." Under Lander's leadership, researchers at the Broad Institute have developed many of the critical new tools needed to understand the molecular basis of human diseases.

In the Classroom

Lander is a professor of biology at MIT and professor of systems biology at Harvard Medical School. He teaches Introduction to Biology at MIT; he also teaches a free online version of the class, MITx: 7.00x Introduction to Biology —The Secret of Life on edX platform.

Genomic Research/Human Genome Project

The Human Genone Project is an international research effort to sequence and map all of the genes —together known as the genome—of members of the Homo sapiens species.

In 1986, Lander attended a meeting at the Cold Spring Harbor Laboratory on Long Island where leading scientists held the first public debate on the idea of mapping the human genome. Lander became a key contributor in the effort to sequence the human genome. He first produced an early genetic map of the whole human genome, showing the positions of about 400 markers—the signposts that geneticists use to locate disease genes on the chromosomes.

In 1990, he received one of the first grants under the NIH's Human Genome Project and founded the WICGR (Whitehead Institute/MIT Center for Genome Research), which was a flagship of the Human Genome Project. Lander was a principal leader of the international Human Genome Project from 1990-2003, with his group being the largest contributor to the mapping and sequencing of the human genetic blueprint.

The Human Genome Project's goal was to provide researchers with the tools to understand the genetic factors in human disease, paving the way for new strategies for their diagnosis, treatment, and prevention. The genome project gave researchers the ability, for the first time, to read nature's complete genetic blueprint for building a human being. As a result, researchers are now able to find a gene suspected of causing an inherited disease in a matter of days, rather than the years it took before the genome sequence was discovered. The Human Genome Project already has fueled the discovery of more than 1,800 disease genes.

Bibliography

Andrew, Lori B. "Gen-Etiquette: Genetic Information, Family Relationships, and Adoption." *Genetic Secrets*, 255–280 (1997).

Watson, James D. "The Human Genome Project: Past, Present, and Future." *Science* 248: 44–49 (April 1990).

Garver, Kenneth L. and Bettylee Garver. "The Human Genome Project and Eugenic Concerns." *American Journal of Human Genetics* 54, no. 1 (January 1994).

Kass, Leon R. *Life, Liberty and the Defense of Dignity: The Challenge for Bioethics*. San Francisco, Calif.: Encounter Books, 2002.

"White House Remarks on Decoding of Genome" (transcript). White House. *New York Times* (June 27, 2000).

Bibliography

By Lander

"Calculating the Secrets of Life: Applications of the Mathematical Sciences in Molecular Biology." *National Academy Press*, 1995 (with Michael S. Waterman).

"Initial sequencing and analysis of the human genome," International Human Genome Sequencing Consortium. *Nature*, 409: 860–921, 2001.

Symmetric Designs: An Algebraic Approach. London Mathematical Society Lecture Note Series (Book 74). Cambridge University Press, 2010.

About Lander

"Eric Lander S. Lander, Ph.D. : Unravelling the Simple, Beautiful Complexity of Life." Academy of Achievement, A Museum of Living History, Washington, D.C., http://www.achievement.org/autodoc/page/lan0bio-1

Kolata, Gina. "Profiles in Science/Eric Lander, Power in Numbers." The *New York Times*, (Jan. 2, 2012).

Hobson, Katherine. *Science Across the Borders. US News & World Report*, (Oct. 30, 2006), and http://www.usnews.com/usnews/news/articles/061022/30lander.htm

(Tsitsi D. Wakhisi)

Joshua Lederberg

Disciplines: Bacteriology, genetics, and medicine

Contribution: Lederberg's extensive work in bacterial genetics established the presence of sexual reproduction among bacteria. He also demonstrated the possibility of genetic manipulation of bacterial genetic material.

May 23, 1925	Born in Montclair, New Jersey
1941	Graduates from Stuyvesant High School in New York City
1942	Enlists in the U.S. Navy, entering a premedical program
1944	Graduates with honors from Columbia University
1944-1946	Attends the College of Physicians and Surgeons at Columbia
1946	Works as a research assistant at Yale University
1947-1958	Serves as assistant professor and professor of genetics at the University of Wisconsin
1948	Receives a Ph.D. from Yale
1958	Awarded the Nobel Prize in Physiology or Medicine
1958-1959	Serves as chair of the genetics department at Wisconsin
1959-1978	Appointed professor of genetics and chair of the genetics department at Stanford
1962	Named director of the Kennedy Laboratories for Molecular Medicine at Stanford
1978-1990	Serves as president of Rockefeller University
1993-1994	Elected president of the New York Academy of Sciences

Early Life

Joshua Lederberg was born on May 23, 1925 in Montclair, New Jersey. His parents, Zvi and Esther Lederberg, had recently emigrated from Palestine. Zvi Lederberg was a rabbi. Lederberg considered himself a precocious youth with an inquiring mind.

He received an excellent education in New York City schools and was given the opportunity to conduct independent research in a laboratory after school hours.

From 1941 to 1944, Lederberg attended Columbia University on a tuition scholarship from the Hayden Trust. He graduated with honors in zoology. Lederberg conducted research and developed an interest in the genetic analysis of plants. He also had the opportunity to discuss genetics with Francis Ryan and to observe his research using the mold *Neurospora*.

In 1942, Lederberg enlisted in the U.S. Navy, where he entered a premedical/medical program designed to train physicians. He was assigned to duty at the St. Albans Naval Hospital on Long Island. In 1944, Lederberg entered the medical school at Columbia University.

Studies in Genetics

Lederberg's desire for a career in research interrupted his medical studies. His interest in genetics led Ryan to suggest that Lederberg contact Edward Lawrie Tatum at Yale University. Tatum and his colleague, George Wells Beadle, were in the process of completing their work on the association of genes with proteins in *Neurospora*. In 1946, Lederberg joined Tatum as a research assistant. That year, he also married Tatum's assistant, Esther Zimmer.

Lederberg's success at Yale brought him an offer from the University of Wisconsin. Despite pejorative references to Lederberg's religion, he accepted a position there as assistant professor of genetics.

Lederberg's successful work on genetic recombination and his demonstration of conjugation, the genetic transfer of deoxyribonucleic acid (DNA), between bacteria, placed him at the forefront of bacterial genetics. By 1954, he had been promoted to full professor. In recognition of his important work, Lederberg, along with Beadle and Tatum, was awarded the 1958 Nobel Prize in Physiology or Medicine.

In 1959, Lederberg accepted an offer to become chair of the new department of genetics at Stanford University. In 1962, he was appointed director of the Kennedy Laboratories for Molecular Medicine at Stanford. He remained in California until 1978, when he was appointed president of Rockefeller University, New York.

Awards and Recognition

Lederberg received numerous awards and honorary degrees. Among his most prized were honorary medical degrees from Tufts University, Massachusetts and the University of Turin, Italy. Ironically, Lederberg never completed his medical studies.

He received the Eli Lilly Award, presented to outstanding young scientists, and the Alexander Hamilton Medal from Columbia University. He also received the National Medal of Science in 1989. He was elected a member of the National Academy of Sciences and the Royal Society of London and served as president of the New York Academy of Sciences in 1993-1994. Lederberg also served as an adviser to the World Health Organization and the National Space Agency.

Bibliography

By Lederberg

"Detection of Biochemical Mutants of Microorganisms," *Journal of Biological Chemistry*, 1946 (with Edward L. Tatum).

"Gene Recombination in *Escherichia coli*," *Nature*, 1946 (with Tatum).

"Gene Recombination in the Bacterium *Escherichia coli*," *Journal of Bacteriology*, 1947 (with Tatum).

"Gene Recombination and Linked Segregations in *Escherichia coli*," *Genetics*, 1947.

Papers in Microbial Genetics: Bacteria and Bacterial Viruses, 1951.

"Replica Plating and Indirect Selection of Bacterial Mutants," *Journal of Bacteriology*, 1952 (with E. M. Lederberg).

"Genetic Exchange in *Salmonella*," *Journal of Bacteriology*, 1952.

"Sex in Bacteria: Genetic Studies, 1945-1952," *Science*, 1954.

"Viruses, Genes, and Cells," *Bacteriological Reviews*, 1957.

Sexual Reproduction in Bacteria

The demonstration of sexual processes in bacteria was instrumental in the development of the field of bacterial genetics.

The role of deoxyribonucleic acid (DNA) as genetic material was first reported in 1944. It was clear that genes must themselves be DNA. Eukaryotic organisms, such as molds, had been demonstrated to carry out sexual reproduction through the exchange of DNA; it was not clear that bacteria could do the same.

Lederberg and Edward Lawrie Tatum initially carried out a number of genetic crosses between different bacterial strains. In doing so, they were able to obtain a new strain that carried genes from each parent. They concluded that bacteria could carry out a form of sexual reproduction called conjugation, the one-way transfer of DNA between bacteria.

Lederberg and Tatum observed that the genetic markers they followed behaved like linked genes; the characteristics mapped in linear order, as would be true if they were aligned along the same chromosome. Lederberg later demonstrated a second means by which genes could transfer between bacteria: transduction. In this process, a virus serves as a vector (carrier) for genetic exchange.

Lederberg's work demonstrated that several methods exist by which bacteria may exchange genetic material. The process of conjugation in particular was later shown to be of particular importance, as genes encoding resistance to antibiotics may also be exchanged among bacteria.

Bibliography

Judson, Horace. *The Eighth Day of Creation*. Cold Spring Harbor, N.Y.: Cold Spring Harbor Press, 1996.

Hayes, William. *The Genetics of Bacteria and Their Viruses*. New York: John Wiley & Sons, 1964.

Stent, Gunther. *Molecular Biology of Bacterial Viruses*. San Francisco: W. H. Freeman, 1963.

Wolstenholme, Gordon., ed. "Biological Future of Man" in *Man and His Future*, 1963.

"Edward Lawrie Tatum," A*nnual Review of Genetics*, 1979.

"Forty Years of Genetic Recombination in Bacteria," *Nature*, 1986.

The Excitement and Fascination of Science: Reflections by Eminent Scientists, vol. 3, 1990 (with others).

Emerging Infections: Microbial Threats to Health in the United States, 1992 (as editor, with Robert E. Shope and Stanley C. Oaks, Jr.).

Encyclopedia of Microbiology, 1992 (as editor).

About Lederberg

Magill, Frank N., ed. "Joshua Lederberg." in *The Nobel Prize Winners: Physiology or Medicine.* Pasadena, Calif.: Salem Press, 1991.

Wasson, Tyler., ed. *Nobel Prize Winners.* Bronx, N. Y: H. W. Wilson, 1987.

McMurray, Emily J., ed. *Notable Twentieth-Century Scientists.* Detroit, Mich.: Gale Research, 1995.

(Richard Adler)

Barbara McClintock

Disciplines: Botany, cell biology, and genetics

Contribution: McClintock proved that genetic recombination involved an exchange of chromosomal material and discovered the existence of mobile genetic elements, called jumping genes.

June 16, 1902	Born in Hartford, Connecticut
1927	Receives a Ph.D. in botany from Cornell University
1931-1933	Given a National Research Council Fellowship
1933	Travels to Germany on a Guggenheim Fellowship
1941	Takes a position at Cold Spring Harbor Laboratory
1944	Elected president of the Genetics Society of America
1944	Named to the National Academy of Sciences
1965-1975	Named Andrew White Professor-at-Large
1967	Wins the Kimber Genetics Award
1970	Awarded the National Medal of Science
1981	Wins the Albert Lasker Basic Medical Research Award
1981	Wins the Wolfe Prize in Medicine
1981	Receives a MacArthur Foundation lifetime annual fellowship
1982	Wins the Horowitz Prize at Columbia University
1983	Wins the Nobel Prize in Physiology or Medicine
Sept. 2, 1992	Dies in Huntington, Long Island

Early Life

Barbara McClintock was the daughter of Thomas McClintock, a physician, and Sara Hardy. Barbara spent considerable time with her paternal aunt and uncle in rural Massachusetts. There, she gained a love for the outdoors. When she was eight years old, her family moved to the Flatbush section of Brooklyn, New York. She enjoyed reading and outdoor sports, including ice skating and bicycle riding. She graduated from the Brooklyn school system in 1918.

Cornell

McClintock enrolled in Cornell University in Ithaca, New York, in 1919 to study biology at the College of Agriculture. She was elected president of the women's freshman class. At Cornell, she studied genetics under C. B. Hutchison and cytology under Lester Sharp. McClintock became interested in the behavior of chromosomes during cell division. She worked with Rollins Emerson, who was studying the genetics of maize (Indian corn). She received her B.S. degree in 1923.

McClintock continued as a graduate student at Cornell, with a major in cytology (the study of cells) and a minor in genetics and zoology. As a graduate student in 1924, she revolutionized the study of maize genetics when she developed a technique to visualize maize chromosomes microscopically. She received her M.A. in 1925 and her Ph.D. in 1927.

Early Research

McClintock continued to study maize while she worked as an instructor of botany at Cornell from 1927 to 1931. She worked with graduate students Marcus Rhoades and George Wells Beadle and became interested in the morphology of maize chromosomes and the correlation of chromosomal morphology with phenotypic traits.

It was during this time that she and Harriet Creighton proved that genetic recombination results from an exchange of chromosomal material during the process of meiosis (gamete formation). McClintock and Creighton published their work in 1931, four months before Curt Stern, a German biologist, published similar findings for *Drosophilia* (the fruit fly).

In 1931, McClintock received a National Research Council Fellowship for two years to study maize. Since Cornell refused to give her an appointment—the university hired women only to teach home economics—she accepted a position as a research fellow at Thomas Hunt Morgan's laboratory at the California Institute of Technology (Caltech).

Between traveling from New York to California, she often spent time at the University of Missouri in Columbia, studying the effects of X-rays on the chromosomes of maize with Lewis Stadler. There, she discovered that when X-rays break chromosomes, the broken ends have a tendency to "find" one another and fuse.

When the chromosomes attempt to separate during meiosis, they break again. She described these events as a breakage-fusion-bridge cycle.

In 1933, McClintock traveled to Germany to work with Richard Goldschmidt on a Guggenheim Fellowship. Adolf Hitler had just become chancellor of Germany, and Nazism was on the rise. After a brief stay with Goldschmidt, she returned to New York to work in Rollins Emerson's maize genetics laboratory at Cornell.

In 1936, the University of Missouri offered McClintock an assistant professorship. She left there in 1941 because the university would not offer her a permanent position because she was a woman.

Transposable Genetic Elements and Crossing-Over

McClintock theorized that some segments of deoxyribonucleic acid (DNA) can move from site to site within a chromosome or between chromosomes. She also offered cytologicai proof that during the formation of gametes, segments of homologous chromosomes can exchange (cross-over), resulting in genetic recombination.

In the 1940s, McClintock noticed that maize plants often contain kernels that are unevenly colored. She discovered that these variegated kernels contain genetic elements that she named dissociation *(Ds)* and activator *(Ac)* that could move (transpose) from one part of the chromosome to another and from one chromosome to another.

Provided that *Ac* is present in the genome, *Ds* can induce chromosome breaks adjacent to its location and move to another location. At its new location, *Ds* may cause a mutation by suppressing genetic activity at that site. *Ds* may then move again, relieving the suppression. Although *Ds* requires *Ac* for movement, *Ac* is capable of autonomous movement.

McClintock realized the implications of her discovery. She thought that the *Ac* and *Ds* genes were controlling genes that could dictate the action of other genes during development. She also realized that mobile genetic elements could be important in evolution, leading to the rapid development of species.

Studies by molecular biologists in the 1980s and 1990s demonstrated that *Ac* is a code for an enzyme called transposase, which is essential for transposition. *Ds* has a similar structure but cannot code for transposase. This is why *Ac* is capable of autonomous transposition but *Ds* requires the presence of *Ac.*

After molecular biologists discovered mobile genetic elements in bacteria in the late 1960s and in *Drosophila* (the fruit fly) and other animals in the 1970s, it became apparent that mobile genetic elements were not an isolated phenomenon specific to maize.

Her work is now known to be of great biological and medical importance, since mobile genetic elements have been shown to cause human disease. The roles of mobile genetic elements in evolution and cell regulation are being determined.

With Harriet Creighton at Cornell University, McClintock also demonstrated that genetic recombination correlates with the exchange of chromosomal material. They designed plants with an unusual ninth chromosome. This unusual chromosome, with a knob at one end and a piece added on the other, carried the dominant gene for colored aleurone and the recessive gene for waxy endosperm. The other ninth chromosome had a normal morphology and carried the recessive gene for colorless aleurone and the dominant gene for starchy endosperm.

These plants were crossed to plants with two normal chromosomes, one carrying the colorless and starchy genes, and the other carrying the colorless and waxy genes. If no genetic recombination occurred,

Cold Spring Harbor Laboratory

In the summer of 1941, McClintock accepted a temporary appointment to study at Cold Spring Harbor Laboratory with Rhoades. Later that Fall, she accepted a staff position there. She would hold this position for the rest of her life. In 1944, she was elected president of the Genetics Society of America; she had been elected vice president in 1931. In 1944, she also became only the third woman to be elected to the National Academy of Sciences, the most prestigious science society in the United States. From 1958 to 1961, she trained Latin American cytologists in maize genetics.

Building on observations made a decade earlier, she spent her early years at the Cold Spring Harbor Laboratory gathering data that suggested the existence of mobile genetic elements. From the early 1940s through the 1950s she developed her theories on mobile genetic elements, which are now called transposable elements and sometimes referred to as jumping genes.

As soon as it was recognized that McClintock's discoveries had broad application, she received numerous awards for her scientific achievements. These awards included the Kimber Genetics Award in 1967, the National Medal of Science in 1970, the Wolf Prize in Medicine in 1981, the Albert Lasker Basic Medical Research Award in 1981, a MacArthur Foundation Fellowship in 1981, the Horowitz Prize of Columbia University in 1982 (shared with Susumu Tonegawa), and the Nobel Prize in Physiology or Medicine in 1983. At the time she was awarded the Nobel Prize, she was only the seventh woman to receive such an award in science and the only sole female recipient in physiology or medicine.

Bibliography

By McClintock

"A Correlation of Cytological and Genetical Crossing-over in *Zea mays*," *Proceedings of the National Academy of Sciences*, 1931 (with Harriet B. Creighton).

"Chromosome Organization and Genic Expression," *Cold Spring Harbor Symposia on Quantitative Biology*, 1951.

the progeny plants would be colorless and starchy, colored and starchy, and colored and waxy. Among the progeny, however, was the genetic recombinant colorless and waxy.

An examination of the ninth chromosome of these recombinant plants revealed a chromosome with only the elongated piece and not the knob, proving that genetic recombination resulted from a physical exchange of chromosome parts.

The cytologicai proof of genetic recombination is one of the major factors resulting in genetic variation and diversity.

Bibliography

Doering, H. P. and P. Starlinger. "Barbara McClintock's Controlling Elements: Now at the DNA Level." *Cell* 39 (1984).

Berg, D. E. and M. M. Howe. *Mobile DNA*. Washington, D.C.: American Society of Microbiology, 1989.

Shapiro, J. A., ed. *Mobile Genetic Elements*: New York: Academic Press, 1983.

Cohen, S. N. and J. A. Shapiro. "Transposable Genetic Elements." *Scientific American* 242 (1980).

Finnegan, D. J. "Transposable Genetic Elements in Eukaryotes." *International Review of Cytology* 93 (1985).

Federoff, N. V. "Transposable Genetic Elements in Maize." *Scientific American* 250 (1984).

About McClintock

Rosser, Sue V. "Barbara McClintock." in *The Nobel Prize Winners: Physiology or Medicine.* Frank N. Magill, ed. Pasadena, Calif.: Salem Press, 1991.

Keller, Evelyn Fox. "Barbara McClintock: The Overlooked Genius of Genetics." in *A Passion to Know: Twenty Profiles in Science.* Allen L. Hammond, ed. New York: Charles Scribner's Sons, 1984.

Keller, Evelyn Fox. *Feeling for the Organism: The Life and Work of Barbara McClintock.* San Francisco, Calif.: W. H. Freeman, 1983.

Lewin, Roger. "A Naturalist of the Genome." *Science* 222 (1983).

Maddux, John. "Nobel Prize to Barbara McClintock." *Nature* 305 (1983).

Wasson, Tyler., ed. *Nobel Prize Winners.* New York: H. W. Wilson, 1987.

McGrayne, Sharon Bertsch. *Nobel Prize Women in Science.* New York: Birch Lane Press, 1993.

(Charles L. Vigue)

Craig Cameron Mello

Areas of Achievement: Molecular medicine

Contribution: Mello was awarded, along with Andrew Z. Fire, the 2006 Nobel Prize for Medicine for the discovering how double-stranded RNA can switch off genes

Oct. 18, 1960	Born in New Haven, Connecticut
1982	Receives B.S. in biochemistry at Brown University, Rhode Island
1990	Completes Ph.D. at Harvard University
1995	Joins the University of Massachusetts Medical School faculty
2000	Named a Howard Hughes Medical Institute investigator
2003	Receives the National Academy of Sciences Award in Molecular Biology
	Receives the Wiley Prize in the Biomedical Sciences
2005	Elected to the National Academy of Sciences
	Receives Lewis S. Rosenstiel Award for Distinguished Work in Medical Research
	Receives the Gairdner Foundation International Award
	Receives the Massry Prize.
2006	Receives the Ludwig Darmstaedter Prize
	Receives the Dr. Paul Janssen Award for Biomedical Research
	Awarded the Nobel Prize in Physiology or Medicine
2008	Receives the Hope Funds Award of Excellence in Basic Research

Early Life

Craig Cameron Mello was born October 18, 1960 in New Haven, Connecticut, where his father, James Mello, was completing a Ph.D. in paleontology at Yale University. His mother, Sally Mello, was an artist. Among Craig Cameron Mello's fondest memories are the field trips he took as a child with his family to Colorado, Wyoming, and the Blue Ridge mountains in Virginia. The youngest of three children, Mello preferred the woods and creeks to the confines of the traditional classroom, a setting where he did not perform well. The eventual Nobel Prize winner enjoyed his hands-on adventures with nature—from searching for fossils to hiking and exploring, all of which predisposed him for a lifelong journey in science.

School Life

The Mello family moved in 1962 to Falls Church in northern Virginia then to Fairfax, Virginia, where Mello attended Fairfax High School. He took all of the science courses offered except advanced physics. After high school, Mello attended Brown University, Rhode Island, where he majored in biochemistry and molecular biology. After graduating in 1982, Mello enrolled at the University of Colorado in Boulder for graduate studies. However, he transferred after just two years to Harvard University, where he received his Ph.D. in 1990. He was a postdoctoral fellow at the Fred Hutchinson Cancer Research Center.

Post Nobel Prize

Today, RNA interference has become the state of the art method by which scientists thwart the expression of specific genes to determine their function. Before RNA interference came to light, Mello studied the mechanisms cells used to differentiate and communicate during the earliest stages of the embryogenesis, a focus that continues in his laboratory today at the University of Massachusetts Medical School, where Mello is a professor in molecular medicine. His research has demonstrated that a cell's position in the embryo can determine what type of tissue it will ultimately become, and he has identified numerous genes involved in determining cell fate in *C. elegans* embryos.

Mello's laboratory is now evenly divided between projects investigating RNA interference and embryonic development, and the two fields continue to converge.

Bibliography

By Mello

"DNA transformation," *Methods In Cell Biology*, 1995 (with Andrew Fire).

"Return to the RNAi world: rethinking gene expression and evolution," *Cell Death & Differation*, 2007.

"Craig C. Mello—Biographical". Nobelprize.org. Nobel Media AB 2013. Web. 3 Sep 2013. http://www.nobelprize.org/nobel_prizes/medicine/laureates/2006/mello-bio.html

About Mello

"UMass Profiles: Research Networking Software," University of Massachusetts Medical School: http://profiles.umassmed.edu/profiles/ProfileDetails.aspx?From=SE&Person=1009

"RNA Interference and Development in C. elegans," Our Scientists, Dr. Craig C. Mello, Howard Hughes Medical Institute, http://www.hhmi.org/scientists/craig-c-mello

Grandin, Karl., ed. *Les Prix Nobel. The Nobel Prizes 2006.* Stockholm, Sweden: Nobel Foundation, 2007.

(Tsitsi D Wakhisi)

Gene Regulation

RNAi drastically changed the way scientists study gene function. Found to be a normal part of gene regulation during embryonic development, it may play a role in cancer and other diseases.

RNA molecules long were thought of as DNA's messengers that carried the genetic code to the cell's protein-building factories. Mello's research showed that certain RNA molecules play a more important role in the cell. He, along with Andrew Z. Fire, then a researcher at the Carnegie Institution of Washington's Department of Embryology, discovered how genes are controlled within living cells. The two collaborated in the late 1980s, experimenting with the roundworm. The two self-described "worm people" continued their long-distance, scientific relationship, later working with the *C. elegans* embryos.

RNA interference works by fooling the cell into destroying the gene's messenger RNA before it can produce a protein. Scientists have speculated that the mechanism developed hundreds of millions of years ago as a way to protect organisms against invading viruses, which sometimes create double-stranded RNA when they replicate. Mello injected RNA into the worms and found that the RNA interference (RNAi) spread from cell to cell throughout the worm's body, regardless of the site of injection, and that the RNA was transmitted from one generation to the next. After further studies conducted in collaboration with Fire, the two scientists revealed in a paper published in *Nature* in 1998 that the gene-silencing effect was in fact caused by double-stranded RNA. Since their discovery, RNA interference has been shown to silence genes in organisms ranging from plants and fruit flies to humans.

Bibliography

Fire, Andrew et al. "Potent and specific genetic interference by double-stranded RNA in Caenorhabditis elegans." *Nature*, 391, 806-811 (19 February 1998), http://www.nature.com/nature/journal/v391/n6669/full/391806a0.html

"Shhhh: Silencing Genes with RNA Interference," *The Scientist*, April 2003, http://www.the-scientist.com/article/display/13678

Greens, Kerry. "Fire and Mello win Nobel Prize: Researchers are honored for discovering the mechanism of RNA interference," *The Scientist*, October 2, 2006, http://www.the-scientist.com/?articles.view/articleNo/24394/title/Fire-and-Mello-win-Nobel-Prize/

Nordqvist, Christian. "Nobel Prize In Medicine For Andrew Fire And Craig Mello," *Medical News Today*, Oct. 3, 2006, http://www.medicalnewstoday.com/articles/53323.php

"Andy Fire and Craig Mello win the Nobel Prize for their work on RNA interference thanks in part to the humble worm, *C. elegans*," The Tech Museum of Innovation. San Jose, Calif., http://genetics.thetech.org/original_news/news34.

Gregor Johann Mendel

Disciplines: Biology and genetics

Contribution: Mendel's experiments demonstrated the manner in which physical traits are inherited from one generation to the next. From his observations two laws that provided the foundation of modern genetics were derived.

July 22, 1822	Born in Heinzendorf, Austria (now Hyncice, Czech Republic)
1840	Begins studies in philosophy at the Olmütz Institute
1843	Enters the Altbrünn Monastery
1845	Begins theological studies at Brünn Theological College
1847	Ordained as a priest
1849	Receives a temporary appointment as a teacher of mathematics and Greek at Znaim High School
1851-1853	Studies physics, chemistry, mathematics, and biology at the University of Vienna
1854	Returns to teaching science in Brünn
1856-1871	Conducts research on inheritance in plants
1867	Sends seed packets to botanist Karl von Nägeli for reproducing his pea experiments
1868	Assumes the position of monastery abbot and gradually ceases his botanical research
Jan. 6, 1884	Dies in Brünn, Austria-Hungary (now Brno, Czech Republic)

Early Life

Johann Mendel was born in Heinzendorf, Austria, on July 22, 1822. Since his father was a peasant farmer with horticultural interests, Mendel spent much of his early life tending plants in the garden and helping in the orchard. After demonstrating academic promise in his elementary education, he was sent away to secondary school, where he completed the curriculum despite illness from poverty-induced nutritional deficiencies.

Although Mendel was a top student, his education would have ended at this point if a falling tree had not disabled his father. Unable to continue farming, his father sold the farm, giving the children substantial portions of the profit. Mendel's sister donated her share to help finance his philosophy studies at the Olmütz Institute.

In 1843, Mendel entered the Augustinian monastery at Brünn, Moravia (later renamed Brno, Czech Republic) and assumed his monastic name of Gregor.

Teaching and the Failed Examination

He obtained a temporary teaching position at a local secondary school in 1849. Although the qualifying examination for a permanent position was ordinarily taken after several years of university study Mendel, without the benefit of a university education, attempted to acquire certification to become a regular teacher the following year. After Mendel failed the examination in the area of natural science, his abbot sent him to the University of Vienna, Austria, where he studied science and mathematics until 1853. Upon completion of his studies, Mendel began teaching science at a high school in Brünn, a profession that he continued until his election as abbot of the monastery in 1868. It is interesting to note that Mendel never gained an official teaching certification.

Mendel and His Peas

Because Mendel had always been curious about the origin of the colors and shapes occurring in the plant world, he acquired a small plot of land in the monastery garden, which he developed into a scientific laboratory to study these characteristics. He chose peas for his study because they were easy to cultivate, readily fertilized one another, and grew rapidly. He grew twenty-two varieties that displayed differences in shape, size, and color. Over a seven-year period, he bred his peas and observed the characteristics of the offspring produced.

In his experiments, Mendel noticed that when two different types of pea were mated, the members of the next generation would all be alike. He called this phenomenon the Law of Uniformity. When one of the uniform offspring was mated to another uniform offspring, the peas produced in the next generation, however, were not uniform. They were split into groups possessing different characteristics according to a definite numerical ratio. This phenomenon he termed the Law of Segregation.

The Laws of Heredity

Mendel mated pure-bred pea plants having easily observable physical traits such as flower color, shape of pea, or height of plant in order to observe the physical characteristics of the offspring.

After Mendel self-pollinated a plant to see the offspring's physical traits, and he then selected a plant with a particular trait such as shape of pea, and artificially mated it with a plant having a different pea shape. He observed that self-pollinated plants with wrinkled peas always bred true (produced offspring with wrinkled peas), while self-pollinated smooth pea plants sometimes bred true and sometimes produced a mixture of smooth-pea offspring and wrinkled-pea offspring.

Crossbreeding a true-breeding smooth-pea plant with a wrinkled-pea plant produced offspring plants that were identical with regard to pea shape: all smooth. This observation led Mendel to propose the Law of Uniformity, which states that the mating of two different types of plants produces offspring in the next generation that are all alike.

In order to determine what had happened to the hereditary factor controlling the wrinkled-pea trait, Mendel allowed members of this first generation to breed with one another, producing a second generation that consisted of a mixture of smooth-pea offspring and wrinkled-pea offspring. Statistically, there were three plants with smooth peas to every plant with wrinkled peas. The trait of wrinkled peas had not been lost in the first generation, only hidden. This observation led Mendel to propose his Law of Segregation, which states that the mating of the uniform offspring will not again produce uniformity, but rather will produce offspring segregated into different forms according to a specific mathematical ratio.

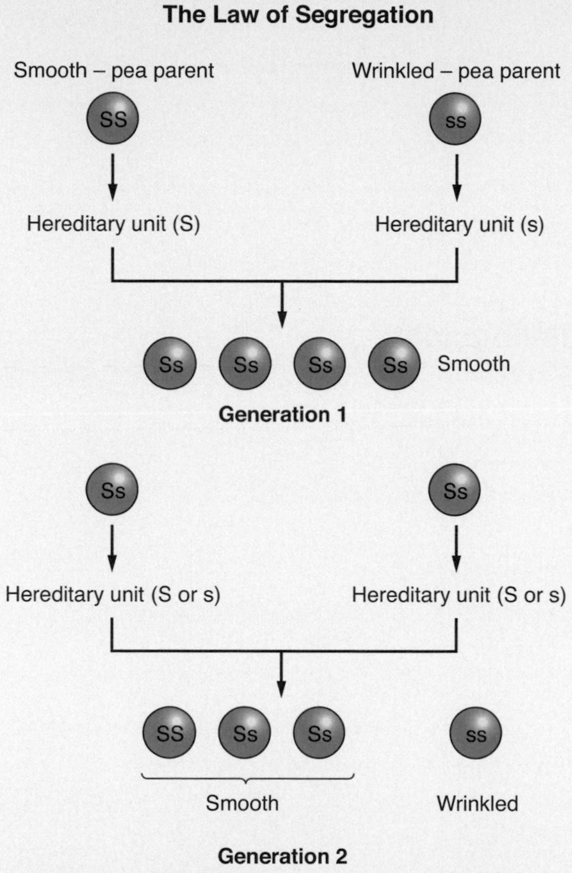

Mendel's Law of Segregation is demonstrated by an initial cross between true-breeding plants with smooth peas and plants with wrinkled peas. The smooth trait is dominant and the wrinkled trait is recessive. The second generation consists of smooth-pea plants and wrinkled-pea plants produced in a ratio of 3:1.

Mendel deduced that every pea plant possesses two heredity units (now known as genes) for pea shape. When bred, each parent plant contributes one of these hereditary units for pea shape to the offspring. He determined that the hereditary unit responsible for the smooth pea (symbolized as S) exerted dominance over the unit responsible for the wrinkled pea (symbolized as s). A pea plant possessing two recessive hereditary units (ss) would have wrinkled peas, while a plant with either two dominant units (SS) or one of each type (Ss) would have smooth peas.

Mendel demonstrated that each parent plant contributes a factor (gene) determining a given trait and that the pairs of factors are not averaged in the offspring. He also demonstrated that a gene-determined trait could disappear in one generation because it was not being expressed and reappear in a later generation.

Mendel's well-designed experiments were the first to focus on the statistical relationships of physical traits produced in the breeding of hybrid plants. Although the significance of his work was not recognized during his lifetime, these experiments provided the foundation on which the modern science of genetics is based.

Bibliography

Corcos, Alain F. and Floyd V. Monaghan. *Gregor Mendel's Experiments on Plant Hybrids.* New Brunswick, N.J.: Rutgers University Press, 1993.

Bateson, William. *Mendel's Principles of Heredity.* Cambridge, England: Cambridge University Press, 1913.

Stern, Curt and Eva Sherwood. *The Origin of Genetics: A Mendel Source Book.* New York: W. H. Freeman, 1966.

Olby, Robert C. *Origins of Mendelism.* Chicago, Ill.: University of Chicago Press, 1985.

Mendel's experiments showed that an averaging of parental characteristics does not occur in the offspring; instead, these characteristics retain their identity. He found that some physical traits are dominant (more likely to be seen in the offspring) and other traits are recessive (less likely to be seen).

Mendel concluded that each parent possesses two factors for a particular trait and that one of these factors is passed on to its offspring. When two different factors are inherited, one from each parent, the dominant factor is the observable one. While the recessive characteristic is not observable, it is still present to be passed on to the next generation. When an offspring obtains a recessive factor from each parent, the recessive physical characteristic again becomes observable.

Mendel Reveals His Work

Mendel described his experiments at the February, 1865, meeting of the Brünn Society for the Study of Natural Science, and presented his conclusions the following month. This work was formally published in 1866 in the society's proceedings as "Versuche über Pflanzenhybriden" (*Experiments in Plant-Hybridisation,* 1910). Mendel's publication had no immediate impact on biological thought, even though it reached the major libraries of Europe and the United States.

Beginning in 1866, Mendel tried to establish a collaboration with noted botanist Karl von Nägeli. In 1867, he sent Nägeli 140 packets of seeds for reproducing his experiments with peas, but the work was never attempted.

Later Life

With his elevation to abbot in 1868, Mendel's life became occupied with administrative duties, leaving little time to pursue scientific interests. In 1874, the Austrian government passed a bill imposing taxation on church properties, and Mendel spent the remaining years of his life fighting this taxation. Although many mourned the death of a beloved, obstinate old priest in January, 1884, no one recognized the passing of a great biologist.

In 1900, three European biologists—Carl Erich Correns, Erich Tschermak von Seysenegg, and Hugo de Vries—independently obtained experimental results similar to those published by Mendel thirty-four years earlier. The acknowledgement of his discovery of the basic laws governing heredity came sixteen years after his death.

Bibliography

By Mendel

"Versuche über Pflanzenhybriden." *Verhandlungen des naturforschenden vereins,* 1866 (*Experiments in Plant-Hybridisation,* 1910).

About Mendel

Iltis, Hugo. *Life of Mendel.* New York: Hafner, 1966.

Thomas, Henry and Dana Lee Thomas. *Living Biographies of Great Scientists.* Garden City, N.Y.: Garden City Books, 1959.

Orel, Vitezslav. *Mendel.* Oxford, England: Oxford University Press, 1984.

(Arlene R. Courtney)

Jacques Lucien Monod

Disciplines: Bacteriology, biology, genetics, and medicine

Contribution: As an early biochemist and molecular biologist, Monod explained how genes are expressed and how gene expression is controlled.

Feb. 9, 1910	Born in Paris, France
1931	Receives a B.A. from the University of Paris
1941	Receives a S.D. degree
1945	Becomes head of a microbial physiology laboratory at the Institut Pasteur in Paris
1954	Becomes head of the cellular biochemistry department at the Institut Pasteur
1959	Named a professor of biochemistry at the University of Paris
1965	Wins the Nobel Prize in Physiology or Medicine with André Lwoff and François Jacob
1967	Appointed a professor of molecular biology at the College de France
1968	Becomes a Fellow of the Salk Institute for Biological Sciences in La Jolla, California
1970	Publishes *Le Hasard et la nécessité* (*Chance and Necessity*, 1971)
1971	Named director of the Institut Pasteur
May 31, 1976	Dies in Cannes, France

Early Life

Jacques Lucien Monod (pronounced "mah-NOH") was born in Paris on February 9, 1910. The Monod family moved to Cannes, in southern France, when he was seven years old. The family was of Swiss origin, except Jacques's mother, Sharlie Todd MacGregor, who was an American of Scottish origin. Consequently, the young boy was exposed to different cultural attitudes within the boundaries of his own family. His father, Lucien, was a talented painter and an avid scholar with tremendous admiration for Charles Darwin. He transmitted this appreciation to his young son, thus instilling in him an interest in biology.

Monod's father played an important role in shaping the young boy's education, introducing him first to music and then to biology. Monod learned to play the cello and thereby gained a love for music. Throughout many of his later years as a molecular biologist, Monod played in a string quartet and directed a Bach choir.

Studies of Bacterial Growth

In his early years as a research scientist, Monod studied bacterial growth, which led him to research into enzyme synthesis.

Monod noted that when two sugars are present in the growth medium, bacterial growth occurs in two phases, separated by a period of no growth. He termed this entire phenomenon "diauxy" (double growth). He guessed, and later established, that the bacteria use different enzymes to metabolize the two sugars.

During the first phase of growth, one sugar is metabolized by enzymes that are always present. When the first sugar is depleted, the bacteria cease growing, and synthesis of the enzymes necessary for metabolism of the second sugar occurs. Monod termed this latter phenomenon enzyme adaptation. During the latency period, the colony is switching from one metabolic program to another.

Monod then focused his attention on enzyme adaptation in order to determine how bacteria adapt to a changing environment when food sources are scarce. He hypothesized that an inducer molecule might serve as an intracellular signal, indicating the availability of a nutrient.

The signaling molecule, or inducer, could possibly bind to a protein that controls gene expression. Such a protein, a repressor, might prevent gene expression unless the inducer binds to it. Binding of the inducer molecular to the repressor would allow gene expression and hence synthesis of the enzymes necessary for metabolism of the second sugar. These ideas, which evolved slowly as a result of discussions with many scientists, proved in essence to be correct.

In 1954, Monod became director of the department of cell biology at the Institut Pasteur. At the same time, he began his collaborative work with François Jacob. These two scientists, together with their students and associates, began studies to understand enzyme adaptation at the molecular level. They wanted to understand the relationship between environmental signals and the genetic apparatus of a bacterial cell.

Monod and Jacob identified a gene cluster which they called an operon. The operon consisted of a regulatory region at the beginning of a deoxyribonucleic acid (DNA) strand, called an operator, followed by a linear string of structural genes, each coding for a different protein. The repressor protein that Monod had earlier hypothesized proved to bind to the operator, thus preventing expression of the operon.

Availability of the appropriate inducer allowed expression of the genes within the operon. Monod and Jacob postulated that expression of the operon resulted in production of a message that allowed synthesis of the newly needed metabolic enzymes. The message proved to be ribonucleic acid (RNA), an intermediate between the DNA genetic material and the proteinaceous enzymes. It was therefore called messenger RNA (mRNA). Thus, the operonic DNA was transcribed to RNA, and the mRNA was translated to protein.

Bibliography

Prescott, Lansing M., John P. Harley, and Donald A. Klein, eds. *Microbiology*. 2d ed. Vol. 1. Dubuque, Iowa: Wm. C. Brown, 1990.

Watson, James D. et al., eds. *Molecular Biology of the Gene*. 4th ed. Menlo Park, Calif.: Benjamin/Cummings, 1987.

University Education

Until 1928, Monod attended the college at Cannes, France. In October of that year, he traveled to Paris to begin studies in biology and chemistry. Later, at the biological station at Roscoff, he was influenced by André Lwoff, who showed him the value of microbiology; by Boris Ephrussi, who introduced him to physiological genetics; and by Louis Rapkine, who convinced him that only a molecular description of life can provide an in-depth picture of living organisms.

In 1936, Ephrussi persuaded Monod to accompany him to the California Institute of Technology (Caltech) in Pasadena, California. There, he would study under the great geneticist Thomas Hunt Morgan. During his stay at Caltech, Monod came to appreciate the full value of free intellectual exchange in a friendly, rather than a hostile or competitive, environment.

In 1938, Monod married Odette Bruhl, an archaeologist and museum curator. They had two sons—one was to become a geologist, the other a physicist. The death of Monod's wife preceded his own by four years.

World War II Efforts

In 1939, war broke out in Europe. In spite of a medical exemption from military service, which allowed him to retain his academic position in Paris, Monod joined the French resistance movement as an officer. His laboratory at the Sorbonne served both as an underground meeting place and as a propaganda print shop.

Although he was captured by the Nazi Gestapo, Monod managed to escape. Subsequently, he continued his resistance efforts. He helped organize the general strike that ultimately led to the liberation of Paris. Monod was eventually honored with several military commendations, including the Croix de Guerre, the Legion of Honor, and the American Bronze Star for his effors during World War II.

Research in Molecular Biology

During his years as a research scientist in Paris, Monod uncovered the molecular nature of the genetic material of living cells. Most importantly, he collaborated with other scientists to discover how genes are organized, how they code for proteins, and how expression of genes is controlled. This work led to the Central Dogma, which states that deoxyribonucleic acid (DNA) is transcribed to ribonucleic acid (RNA) and that RNA is translated to protein.

The importance of Monod's studies gradually began to be recognized. In 1959, he became a professor of biochemistry at the University of Paris, while retaining his post at the Institut Pasteur. Following his receipt of the Nobel Prize in Physiology or Medicine in 1965, he became director of the Institut Pasteur.

Philosophy

Monod used his fame and influence to bolster the cause of basic research. The French government favored directed research with evident applicability to medicine or industry. Monod pointed out that his basic research activities, conducted with little government support from France, had led to an understanding of heredity and disease. Without sup port from private sources and the United States, his contributions would have been impossible.

Monod declared that modern science had paved the way to a new moral rationalism based on "logic confronted with experience." In 1970 he published *Le Hasard et la nécessité* (*Change and Necessity*, 1971), which became an immediate bestseller. In this book, he pondered the philosophical implications of discoveries concerning basic life processes. He expressed the opinion that life arose as a result of chance events that were shaped by the need for survival.

Monod concluded that, "Man knows at last that he is alone in the indifferent immensity of the universe. His duty, like his fate, is written nowhere.

It is for him to choose between the kingdom and the darkness." He believed that nationalism and war are parts of the "darkness," while universal cooperation and reason are to be found in the "kingdom."

Monod died in 1976 at the age of sixty-six.

Bibliography

By Monod

Recherches sur la croissance de cultures bacteriennes, 1942.

"Genetic Regulatory Mechanisms in the Synthesis of Proteins," *Journal of Molecular Biology*, 1961 (with François Jacob).

From Biology to Ethics, 1969.

Le Hasard et la nécessité: Essai sur la philosophic naturelle de la biologie moderne, 1971 (*Chance and Necessity: An Essay on the Natural Philosophy of Modern Biology*, 1971).

About Monod

Magill, Frank N., ed."Jacques Lucien Monod." in *The Nobel Prize Winners: Physiology or Medicine*. Pasadena, Calif.: Salem Press, 1991.

"Jacques Monod, 1910-1976." *Nature* (1976).

Lwoff, André and Agnes Ullmann, eds. *Origins of Molecular Biology: A Tribute to Jacques Monod*. Paris: Academic Press, 1979.

(Milton H. Saier, Jr.)

Thomas Hunt Morgan

Disciplines: Biology, genetics, and zoology

Contribution: The most famous geneticist of the early part of the twentieth century, Morgan established the fruit fly, *Drosophila melanogaster*, as a preeminent experimental organism. All of the major principles of transmission genetics were developed in his fly laboratory in the period from 1908 to 1926.

Sept. 25, 1866	Born in Lexington, Kentucky
1886	Earns a B.S. from the State College of Kentucky
1890	Awarded a Ph.D. from The Johns Hopkins University
1891	Appointed associate professor of biology at Bryn Mawr College, Pennsylvania
1904	Appointed professor of experimental zoology at Columbia University
1908	Begins work with *Drosophila*
1927-1928	Serves as president of the National Academy of Sciences
1928	Moves to the California Institute of Technology (Caltech) as head of the biology division
1929	Serves as president of the American Association for the Advancement of Science
1933	Awarded the Nobel Prize in Physiology or Medicine
1939	Receives the Copley Medal of the Royal Society
1942	Retires from Caltech
Dec. 4, 1945	Dies in Pasadena, California

Early Life

Thomas Hunt Morgan was born in Lexington, Kentucky, in 1866, the same year that Gregor Mendel published his observations on inheritance in the garden pea, and the new science of genetics was born. The great-grandson of Francis Scott Key, Morgan was a member of a prominent aristocratic family. He developed a passion for the study of living things early in his life through his boyhood nature collections, and he later pursued a four-year program in natural history at the State College of Kentucky.

Morgan began graduate study at The Johns Hopkins University in 1886, and it was there that he developed a lifelong commitment to experimental laboratory research and a hands-on experimental approach to teaching. His research at this time focused on aspects of embryology and regeneration. After receiving his doctorate in 1890, Morgan joined the faculty of Bryn Mawr College, Pennsylvania, as an associate professor of biology.

Bryn Mawr College

While Morgan was not a polished classroom lecturer, he excelled in the research laboratory, where he was always willing to provide instruction to students who were sufficiently adept to keep up with him. Possessing an acute scientific curiosity, Morgan worked with more than fifty different experimental organisms during the course of his professional life. He was one of the first scientists to demonstrate parthenogenesis (the development of an unfertilized egg) in sea urchins, and he studied the regeneration of lost or injured body parts in flatworms, jellyfish, starfish, and other marine organisms.

In 1900, Morgan returned to Naples, Italy, where he had previously spent a year as a research scientist. This was just after the rediscovery of Mendel's work, and discussion there among the world's greatest biologists focused on heredity, mutation, and Charles Darwin's views on evolution. From this point on, Morgan's primary research concerns were centered on aspects of genetics and evolution, and their relationship to the phenomenon of mutation.

Columbia University and the "Fly Room"

In 1904, Morgan married Lilian Vaughan Simpson, a graduate of Bryn Mawr and an accomplished biologist in her own right. They moved to New York City, where, at Columbia University, he became the country's first professor of experimental zoology. In addition to his interests in genetics and evolution, Morgan still pursued experimental work in development, embryology, and the mechanism of sex determination.

In 1908, Morgan had a graduate student work on what was to be a failed project on eye development in the fruit fly, *Drosophila melanogaster*. Morgan found, however, that the *Drosophila* stocks were easy to maintain in the laboratory, and he began to look for natural variation and new mutant characteristics in this tiny organism.

Sex-Linked Genes and Chromosome Maps

Morgan discovered sex-linkage, a pattern of inheritance found only when a gene is located on the X chromosome. Crosses between several different mutant types showing this distinctive inheritance allowed him to construct the first genetic map.

Unlike Gregor Mendel's pea plants, the chromosomes in most animals, including fruit flies and humans, are either sex chromosomes (those involved in sex determination) or autosomes. Fruit flies have one pair of sex chromosomes—two X chromosomes for

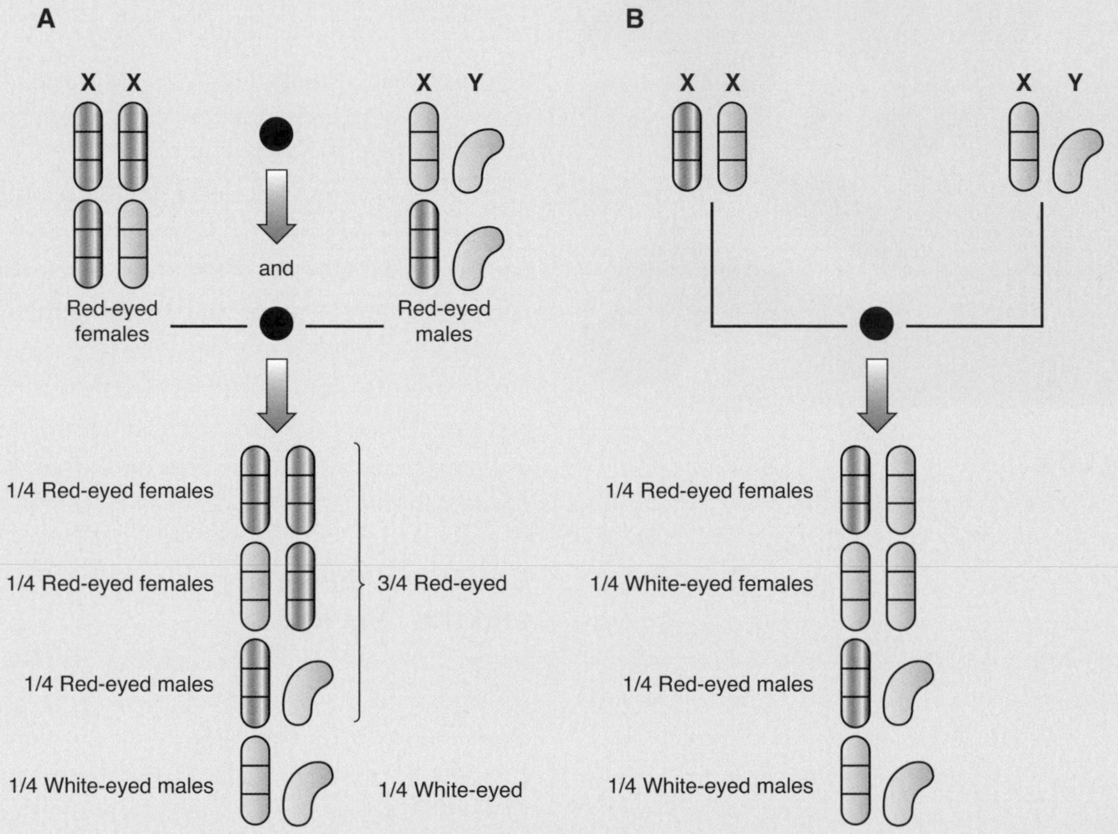

A: A red-eyed female is crossed with a white-eyed male. The red-eyed progeny interbreed to produce offspring in a ¾ red to ¼ white ratio. All the white-eyed flies are male. B: A white-eyed male is crossed with its red-eyed daughter, giving red-eyed and white-eyed males and females in equal proportions.

females, and an X chromosome and a Y chromosome for males—and three pairs of autosomes. Genes for body functions or structures unrelated to sex determination can be located on the X chromosome, and the first of these to be described was Morgan's white-eyed (w) *Drosophila* mutant.

When Morgan mated this white-eyed male with a red-eyed female, he found that all the progeny flies were red-eyed. He allowed these progeny flies to interbreed freely and noted that their offspring appeared in an approximate 3:1 ratio, red-eyed to white-eyed. This result was consistent with Mendelian inheritance, except that all the white-eyed flies in this second generation were male. When white-eyed males were crossed with their red-eyed daughters, the progeny consisted of approximately $1/4$ red-eyed females, $1/4$ red-eyed males, $1/4$ white-eyed females, and $1/4$ white-eyed males.

Morgan interpreted his data by suggesting that the gene for eye color is on the X chromosome and that no equivalent gene exists on the Y chromosome (which is much smaller than the X). Thus, females would have two copies of the gene, whereas males would have only one. A single copy of the white-eye gene will cause the white-eye mutation in males, but females would need two copies of the recessive white-eye gene (one on each of the two X chromosomes) in order to express the trait. The crosses that Morgan performed and his interpretations are shown in the accompanying figure.

Other mutant characters showing sex-linked inheritance were soon discovered, including miniature wing (m) and yellow body (y). Morgan crossed a white-eyed, miniature-winged female with a male showing both of these dominant traits. As expected, all the male progeny showed both mutant traits, while the females had red eyes and large wings. When these were interbred, Morgan found that 63.1 percent of the offspring showed either both mutant traits or both normal traits (parental types). The remaining 36.9 percent, however, showed either white eyes or miniature wings, but not both (recombinant types).

Similar crosses involving flies with the white-eye and yellow-body traits resulted in 98.7 percent parental types and only 1.3 percent recombinant types. Morgan thus concluded that the genes for white eyes and yellow bodies are very close to each other on the X chromosome and are therefore much less likely to be separated by a genetic exchange (cross-over) than are the genes for white eyes and miniature wings, which are separated by a greater physical distance. Morgan constructed the first chromosome map using the X chromosome in *Drosophila*, with the genes w and m separated by 36.9 map units (now called morgans) and w and y separated by only 1.3 morgans.

The discovery of sex-linkage was the conclusive evidence in support of the chromosome theory of heredity. With the procedures developed by Morgan and his colleagues, genetic maps have been constructed for thousands of experimental organisms and they remain one of the most basic and useful tools for genetic analysis.

Bibliography

Russell, Peter. *Genetics*. Boston, Mass.: Scott, Foresman, 1995.

Hunt, Thomas Morgan et al. *The Mechanism of Mendelian Heredity*. New York: Henry Holt, 1915.

Hunt, Thomas Morgan and Calvin B. Bridges. *Sex-Linked Inheritance in* Drosophila. Washington, D.C.: Carnegie Institute, 1916.

In May, 1910, Morgan found a striking new fly in his stocks—a white-eyed mutant—startlingly distinct from the other flies with deep red eyes. His elegant and detailed genetic analysis of the transmission of this mutant trait established the phenomenon of sex-linkage and led to the first assignment of a particular gene (white eye) to a particular chromosome (the X chromosome).

In the following years, dozens of new mutant flies showing variations in wing shape or vein pattern, body shape or color, eye shape or color, and bristle number or pattern were described, and the responsible genes were identified and mapped on one of the four chromosome pairs in *Drosophila*. Morgan coined the terms "linkage" and "crossing-over," and the units of physical distance between genes on chromosome maps are now called "morgans" in his honor.

In 1915, Morgan and three of his former students—Alfred H. Sturtevant, Calvin B. Bridges, and Hermann Joseph Muller—wrote *The Mechanism of Mendelian Heredity*. This work became the classic textbook for the new generation of geneticists new observations from the "fly room" emerged regularly over the next decade, resulting in the understanding of other features of transmission genetics, including multiple alleles and nondisjunction.

The California Institute of Technology

In 1928, Morgan left Columbia to become the head of the biology division of the California Institute of Technology (Caltech). His mission was to organize and direct a completely new school of biology. He emphasized genetics and evolution, along with embryology, physiology, biophysics, and biochemistry; and he successfully recruited one of the most talented groups of biologists ever to work together at a single institution.

In 1933, Morgan was awarded the Nobel Prize in Physiology or Medicine for his work on the chromosome theory of inheritance, the first geneticist to be so honored. He continued his personal research up until the time of his retirement from Caltech at the age of seventy-six. He died three years later in Pasadena, California.

Bibliography

By Morgan

The Development of the Frog's Egg: An Introduction to Experimental Embryology, 1897.

Regeneration, 1901.

Evolution and Adaptation, 1903.

Experimental Zoology, 1907.

Heredity and Sex, 1913.

The Mechanism of Mendelian Heredity, 1915 (with Alfred H. Sturtevant, Hermann Joseph Muller, and Calvin B. Bridges).

A Critique of the Theory of Evolution, 1916.

The Genetic and the Operative Evidence Relating to Secondary Sexual Characters, 1919.

Some Possible Bearings of Genetics on Pathology, 1922.

The Third Chromosome Group of Mutant Characters of Drosophila Melanogaster, 1923 (with Bridges).

Laboratory Directions for an Elementary Course in Genetics, 1923 (with Muller, Sturtevant, and Bridges).

Human Inheritance, 1924.

"The Genetics of *Drosophila*," *Bibliographia Genetica*, 1925 (with Bridges and Sturtevant).

Experimental Embryology, 1927.

What Is Darwinism?, 1929.

The Scientific Basis of Evolution, 1932.

Embryology and Genetics, 1934.

About Morgan

Allen, Garland E. *T H. Morgan: The Man and His Science*. Princeton, N.J.: Princeton University Press, 1978.

Shine, Ian and Sylvia Wrobel. *Thomas Hunt Morgan, Pioneer of Genetics*. Lexington, Ky.: University Press of Kentucky, 1976.

(Jeffrey A. Knight)

Hermann Joseph Muller

Disciplines: Biology, cell biology, and genetics

Contribution: Muller discovered the phenomenon of mutagenesis and designed an experiment that proved that new genetic mutations could be induced by radiation (X-rays).

Dec. 21, 1890	Born in New York City
1910	Earns a B.A. from Columbia University
1915	Awarded a Ph.D. from Columbia
1915	Serves as assistant professor of biology at the William Marsh Rice Institute in Houston, Texas
1918	Named assistant professor of zoology at Columbia
1920	Moves to the University of Texas in Austin
1932	Awarded a Guggenheim Fellowship for study in Berlin
1933	Becomes a research scientist at the Institute of Genetics in Leningrad, Soviet Union
1937	Moves to the Institute of Animal Genetics at the University of Edinburgh, Scotland
1940	Returns to the United States to teach at Amherst College
1945	Named a professor of zoology at Indiana University
1946	Receives the Nobel Prize in Physiology or Medicine
1949	Acts as president of the American Society of Human Genetics
1964	Retires from Indiana University
Apr. 5, 1967	Dies in Indianapolis, Indiana

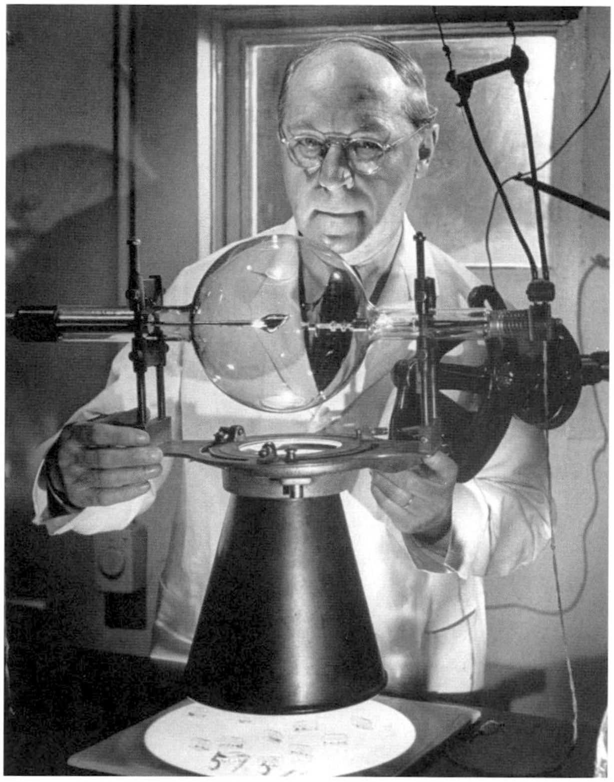

Early Life

Growing up in Manhattan, Hermann Joseph Muller developed an inquiring mind. He excelled as an undergraduate at Columbia University and was handpicked by Thomas Hunt Morgan to pursue graduate work in his laboratory.

As a member of the group studying the fruit fly (*Drosophila melanogaster*) in Morgan's "fly room," Muller became a major contributor to the chromosome theory of heredity. He was a coauthor of the first great textbook of modern genetics, *The Mechanism of Mendelian Heredity* (1915), with Morgan, Alfred H. Sturtevant, and Calvin B. Bridges.

Muller's early work with fruit flies was on "chief" genes and modifiers. These are more complex examples of Mendelian inheritance, involving two or more genes for a single trait. His elucidation of the inheritance patterns helped to restore faith in Darwinism, since it provided a genetic basis for the small fluctuations in character variation necessary to serve as the raw material for natural selection.

The Induction of Mutations by X-Rays

Muller demonstrated that X-rays could alter genes permanently, resulting in the production of new, heritable mutations. Radiation was the first physical or chemical mutagen to be discovered.

Muller performed three quite different experiments using three distinct genetic strategies in the fruit fly, *Drosophila melanogaster*, to demonstrate the mutagenic effects of X-rays. One of these is shown in some detail in the accompanying diagram.

Muller took male flies exhibiting the sex-linked recessive trait of bobbed bristles and subjected them to varying doses of X radiation. These flies were mated to

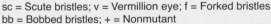

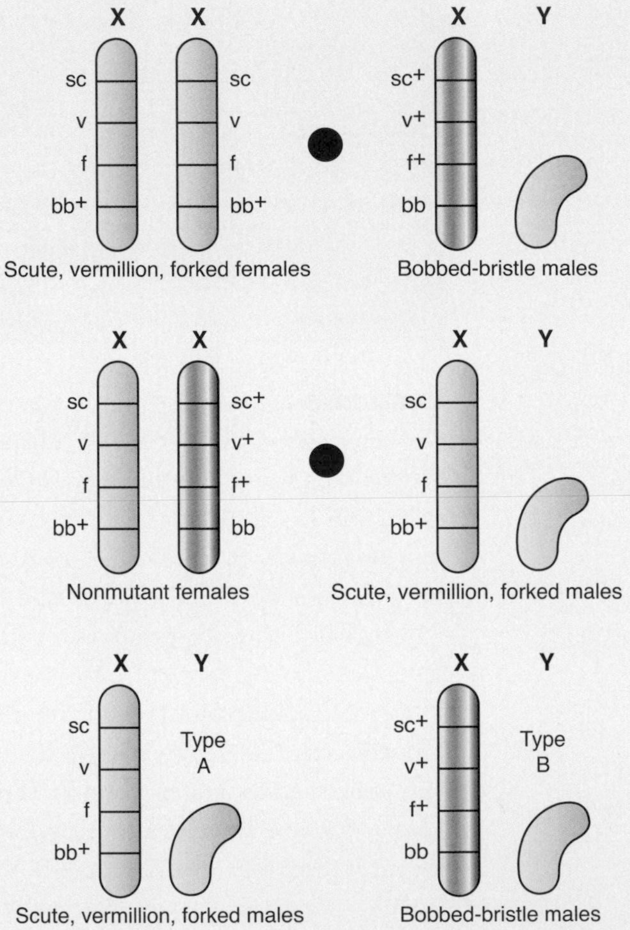

sc = Scute bristles; v = Vermillion eye; f = Forked bristles
bb = Bobbed bristles; + = Nonmutant

If, for a given fly and its descendants, an induced or spontaneous lethal mutation occurs in the paternal X chromosome (shaded), no third-generation males of type B will result. If a spontaneous lethal mutation occurs in an original maternal X chromosome, then no third-generation males of type A will result.

females showing three different sex-linked recessive mutations. As expected, all the female progeny were nonmutant in appearance. The sons of many such females were then closely examined.

If the X-rays had induced a recessive lethal mutation somewhere on the X chromosome in the sperm cells of the irradiated males, then no males showing bobbed bristles should result in the final mating. Conversely, if there were a spontaneous lethal mutation in the maternally derived X chromosome, all the males from the final mating should show bobbed bristles. Muller found that as the X-ray dosage increased, so did the mutation frequency, and essentially all the new mutants were of paternal origin.

The change in mutation frequency was dramatic—a 15,000 percent increase over spontaneous rates when X-rays were used. The X-rays were also shown to induce many new visible mutations. From 1910 to 1926, about 200 different mutations had been found by all *Drosophila* workers combined; using X-rays, Muller found half that number by himself in fewer than two months.

Muller's outspoken warnings concerning the mutagenic dangers of radiation were instrumental to the more conservative use of X-rays in medicine and ultimately to the development of the international nuclear test ban treaty.

Bibliography

Muller, Hermann Joseph. "Artificial Transmutation of the Gene." *Science* 66 (1927).

Carlson, Elof Axel. *Genes, Radiation, and Society: The Life and Work of H. J. Muller*. Ithaca, N.Y.: Cornell University Press, 1981.

Griffiths, Anthony et al. *An Introduction to Genetic Analysis*. New York: W. H. Freeman, 1993.

Mutation Studies

In 1920, Muller accepted a position as assistant professor of zoology at the University of Texas in Austin. He believed that the major problems in transmission genetics had been solved, since the chromosome theory and Mendelism had successfully merged. He also believed that the future of genetics lay in a new direction—a focus on the nature of the gene and the nature of mutation.

Muller began working with radium and X-rays, and he developed an international reputation in 1927 when he presented his work on X-ray-induced mutations at the Fifth International Congress of Genetics in Berlin, Germany. He showed not only that single gene mutations were induced by radiation but that macrolesions (chromosome breaks and rearrangements) could also result.

To the U.S.S.R. and Back

Muller developed a social idealism as a youth that led to his acceptance of communism under Vladimir Ilich Lenin as an effective approach for addressing poverty, racial prejudice, and worker exploitation. Depressed by a failing marriage, conflicts with his colleagues in Texas, and harassment by the Federal Bureau of Investigation (FBI), Muller left Texas in 1932 to study in Berlin on a Guggenheim Fellowship. He moved to the Institute of Genetics in Leningrad the following year and remained in the Soviet Union until 1937.

Witnessing at first hand the horrors of the police state under Joseph Stalin and the destruction of the study of genetics in the Soviet Union with the rise to power of Trofim Lysenko, Muller left in despair in 1937. He renounced communism as a political system, and, after brief stints at the University of Edinburgh, Scotland and Amherst College in Massachusetts, he settled into what would be his most permanent position as professor of zoology at Indiana University.

The Nobel Prize

Muller continued his studies on mutation and mutagenesis and in 1946 won the Nobel Prize in Physiology or Medicine for his work on X-rays as a mutagen (mutation-causing agent). He was committed to the social implications and applications of his work, and he used his fame as a Nobel laureate to educate the public about the dangers of radiation.

In other areas of social reform, Muller met with mixed success. He championed sexual equality, day care, and positive eugenics, advocating sperm banks and artificial insemination as voluntary reproductive options. He was an atheist and a humanist who believed that humans had the right to plan their own destiny.

Muller retired from Indiana University in 1964 and died in 1967 in Indianapolis at the age of seventy-six.

Bibliography

By Muller

The Mechanism of Mendelian Heredity, 1915 (with Thomas Hunt Morgan, Alfred H. Sturtevant, and Calvin B. Bridges).

"Artificial Transmutation of the Gene," *Science*, 1927.

"The Production of Mutations by X-Rays," *Proceedings of the National Academy of Sciences*, 1928.

Out of the Night: A Biologist's View of the Future, 1935.

Bibliography on the Genetics of Drosophila, 1939.

Genetics, Medicine, and Man, 1947 (with C. C. Little and L. H. Snyder).

Hollaender, A., ed. "The Nature of the Genetic Effects Produced by Radiation" and "The Manner of Production of Mutations by Radiation" in *Radiation Biology*, 1954.

"Radiation and Human Mutation," *Scientific American*, 1955.

Studies in Genetics: The Selected Papers of H. J. Muller, 1962.

About Muller

Grosch, D. S. and L. E. Hopwood. *Biological Effects of Radiations*. New York: Academic Press, 1979.

Carlson, Elof Axel. *Genes, Radiation, and Society: The Life and Work of H. J. Muller*. Ithaca, N.Y.: Cornell University Press, 1981.

Magill, Frank N., ed. "Hermann Joseph Muller." in *The Nobel Prize Winners: Physiology or Medicine*. Pasadena, Calif.: Salem Press, 1991.

Nobel Lectures in Molecular Biology, 1933-1975. New York: Elsevier, 1977.

(Jeffrey A. Knight)

Marshall W. Nirenberg

Disciplines: Biology, cell biology, chemistry, and genetics

Contribution: Nirenberg is the scientist most responsible for deciphering the genetic code.

Apr. 10, 1927	Born in New York City
1948	Earns a B.S. from the University of Florida, Gainesville
1952	Receives an M.S. in biology from the University of Florida
1957	Earns a Ph.D. in biochemistry from the University of Michigan, Ann Arbor
1957	Begins research at the National Institutes of Health (NIH) in Bethesda, Maryland
1960	Appointed a research biochemist at NIH
1965	Presented with the National Medal of Science by President Lyndon B. Johnson
1966	Appointed Chief of Biochemical Genetics at the National Heart, Lung, and Blood Institute of NIH
1967	Elected to the National Academy of Sciences
1968	Awarded the Nobel Prize in Physiology or Medicine
1992	Becomes a signatory to the World Scientists' Warning to Humanity, concerning dangers to the natural environment from human activity

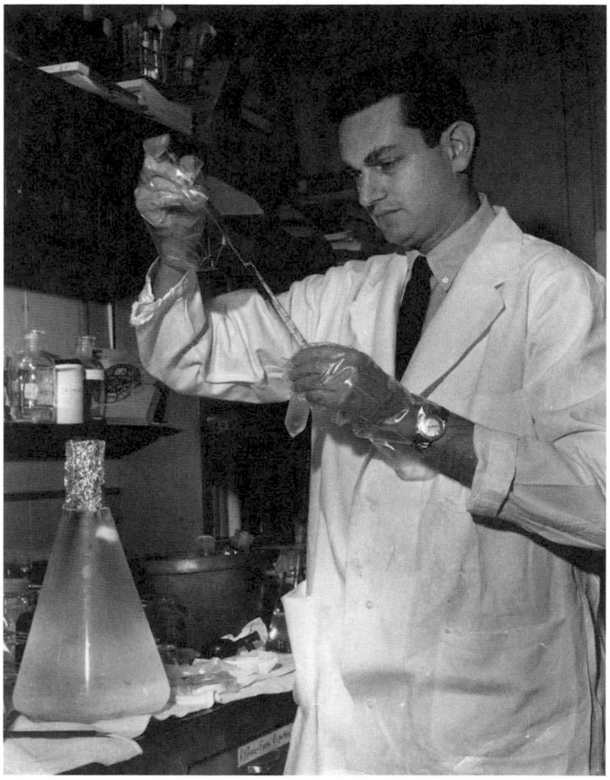

Early Life

Marshall Warren Nirenberg was born in New York City on April 10, 1927 to Harry and Minerva Nirenberg.

When he was ten years old his family moved to Orlando, Florida. Nirenberg soon came to consider himself a Floridian.

In 1944, he enrolled at the University of Florida, studying zoology and botany—subjects that had long interested him. While still an undergraduate, he worked as a laboratory assistant and also as a teaching assistant. Working in the nutrition laboratory, he was introduced to biochemistry, which was little studied at the time by undergraduates. Nirenberg learned how to use radioactive isotopes to follow the course of biochemical reactions, a technique that was to prove vital to his later research.

Nirenberg graduated in 1948 but stayed on for graduate studies in biology, continuing to work in the nutrition laboratory.

The Genetic Code

Nirenberg found that the structures and properties of proteins are controlled by the sequence of bases in deoxyribonucleic acid (DNA) and ribonucleic acid (RNA).

Proteins are very large, complex molecules that direct the vast array of chemical reactions occurring within living organisms and that constitute the life of those organisms. Many structural components of organisms are also proteins. The DNA in any living thing determines what kinds of proteins its cells can make, and thus what kind of organism it is: ant or oak tree, man or woman, and so on.

All protein molecules consist of very long chains of simple components called amino acids. There are only twenty types of amino acid in proteins, but the different orders in which they can be arranged in the chain give rise to many sorts of protein, with very different biochemical properties. DNA contains the instructions, in coded form, for assembling amino acids into proteins in the right order, but DNA does not control protein production directly. When needed, its code is copied into a related substance called RNA. This comes in three forms: ribosomal RNA (rRNA), which forms ribosomes, the intracellular bodies where proteins are actually assembled; transfer RNA (tRNA), which carries the amino acids to the ribosomes; and messenger RNA (mRNA), which carries the actual instructions for protein assembly.

RNA, like DNA, is itself a long chain molecule, and it is the order of the components called bases in the mRNA chain that codes for the order of amino acids in the protein. The bases may be considered as the letters in which the code is written, but there are only four types of bases: adenine (A), guanine (G), cytosine (C), and uracil (U). Therefore, it takes a "word," or codon, consisting of three bases, in a particular order, to specify a particular amino acid.

This much was suspected, if not yet proven, when Nirenberg began his work, but it was not known which codons specified which particular amino acids. When Nirenberg and J. Heinrich Matthaei added an artificial mRNA containing only the base uracil to their bacterial extract—containing ribosomes, tRNA, free amino acids, and other necessary components—they found that an unnatural protein chain was produced containing only the amino acid phenylalanine. Thus, UUU is the code word for phenylalanine.

Further experiments followed with other artificial mRNAs, but it was not then known how to make long artificial RNA chains with different bases in a particular order, so it was impossible to solve much of the code in this way. Nirenberg and Philip Leder found, however, that RNA chains only three base units long (single codons, in effect), which could be made with bases in a specific order, would cause tRNA carrying the appropriate amino acid to stick fast to the ribosomes. These ribosomes were then filtered out, and the particular amino acid stuck to them could be identified by standard radioactive isotope techniques. The entire code was quickly deciphered.

Bibliography

Woese, Carl R. *The Genetic Code*. New York: Harper & Row, 1967.

Nirenberg, Marshall. "The Genetic Code: II." *Scientific American* (March, 1963).

Watson, James D. *The Molecular Biology of the Gene*. 4th ed. Menlo Park, Calif.: Benjamin/Cummings, 1987.

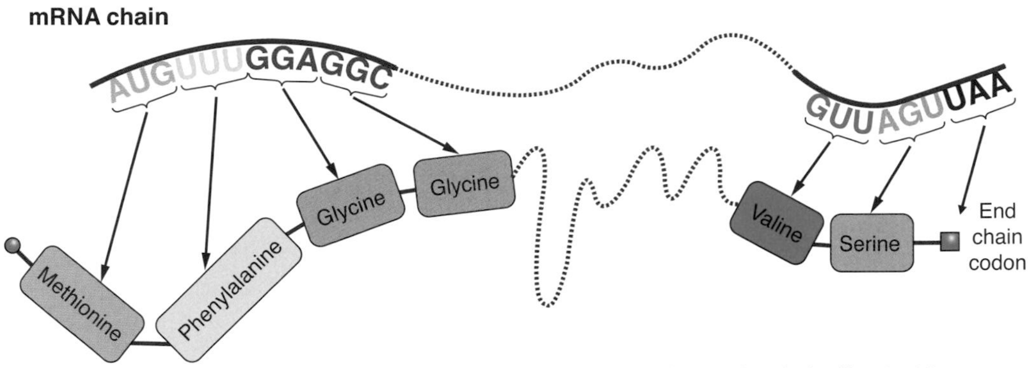

Protein synthesis is directed by messenger RNA (mRNA). The order of the amino acids in the protein chain is controlled by the order of the bases in the mRNA chain. It takes a codon of three bases to specify one amino acid.

The Full Genetic Code

First row ↓ / Second row →	U	C	A	G	Third row ↓
U	Phenylalanine Phenylalanine Leucine Leucine	Serine Serine Serine Serine	Tyrosine Tyrosine END CHAIN END CHAIN	Cysteine Cysteine END CHAIN Tryptophan	U C A G
C	Leucine Leucine Leucine Leucine	Proline Proline Proline Proline	Histidine Histidine Glutamine Glutamine	Arginine Arginine Arginine Arginine	U C A G
A	Isoleucine Isoleucine Isoleucine Methionine	Threonine Threonine Threonine Threonine	Asparagine Asparagine Lysine Lysine	Serine Serine Arginine Arginine	U C A G
G	Valine Valine Valine Valine	Alanine Alanine Alanine Alanine	Aspartic acid Aspartic acid Glutamic acid Glutamic acid	Glycine Glycine Glycine Glycine	U C A G

The amino acid specified by any codon can be found by looking for the wide row designated by the first base letter of the codon shown on the left, then the column designated by the second base letter along the top, and finally the narrow row marked on the right, in the appropriate wide row, by the third letter of the codon. Many amino acids are represented by more than one codon. The codons UAA, UAG, and UGA do not specify an amino acid but instead signal where a protein chain ends.

Nirenberg's master's thesis dealt with the classification and ecology of caddis flies. In 1952, he began his doctoral study in biochemistry at the University of Michigan. His doctoral thesis concerned the uptake of sugars by cancer cells, and he afterward received a fellowship from the American Cancer Society for research at the National Institutes of Health (NIH), in Bethesda, Maryland. In 1960, he was appointed to the regular staff there.

Cracking the Code

Shortly after this appointment, Nirenberg began to collaborate with German scientist J. Heinrich Matthaei. They prepared an extract from bacterial cells that could make protein even when no intact living cells were present. Adding an artificial form of ribonucleic acid (RNA), polyuridylic acid, to this extract caused it to make an unnatural protein composed entirely of the amino acid phenylalanine. This provided the first clue to the code through which RNA—and, ultimately deoxyribonucleic acid (DNA)—control the production of specific types of protein in living cells.

Nirenberg announced these results at the Fifth International Congress of Biochemistry in Moscow, U.S.S.R., in August, 1961. As an unknown scientist with an obscurely titled paper, his initial talk was very poorly attended. He was asked to repeat it, however, for the final session of the full congress. Some listeners recall being "electrified" by what they heard, although others (apparently) slept through it.

Over the next few years, many similar experiments were done, by Nirenberg and others, using different forms of synthetic RNA to stimulate protein production. Only modest further progress could be made, however, in deciphering the code by such methods.

In 1964, Nirenberg announced that he and Philip Leder had devised a new, more powerful decoding technique. Within a year, the genetic code was fully deciphered.

After the Code

A shy, unassuming man, Nirenberg gained a reputation for total dedication to his science. In 1966, he was appointed Chief of Biochemical Genetics at the National Heart, Lung, and Blood Institute. In 1968, he shared the Nobel Prize in Physiology or Medicine with Har Gobind Khorana and Robert Holley. He has continued to work on the very complex problems of understanding how genetic information controls the development and metabolism of living organisms.

Bibliography

By Nirenberg

"The Dependence of Cell-Free Protein Synthesis in *E. coli* upon Naturally Occurring or Synthetic Polyribonucleotides," *Proceedings of the National Academy of Sciences of the United States*, 1961 (with J. Heinrich Matthaei).

"The Genetic Code: II," *Scientific American*, 1963.

"RNA Codewords and Protein Synthesis: The Effect of Trinucleotides upon the Binding of sRNA to Ribosomes," *Science*, 1964 (with Philip Leder).

About Nirenberg

Judson, Horace Freeland. *The Eighth Day of Creation: The Makers of the Revolution in Biology*. New York: Simon & Schuster, 1979.

Magill, Frank N., ed. "Marshall W. Nirenberg." in *The Nobel Prize Winners: Physiology or Medicine*. Pasadena, Calif.: Salem Press, 1991.

"Nirenberg, Marshall W(arren)." in *Current Biography Yearbook*. New York: H. W. Wilson, 1965.

(Nigel J. T. Thomas)

Reginald Crundall Punnett

Disciplines: Biology, genetics, and zoology

Contribution: Punnett performed numerous breeding experiments that helped establish Mendelian genetics as a new field in biology.

June 20, 1875	Born in Kent, England
1889	Awarded a scholarship to Caius College, University of Cambridge
1899-1902	Serves as a demonstrator in natural history at the University of St. Andrews, Scotland
1901	Elected a Fellow of Caius College
1902	Becomes a demonstrator in zoology at Cambridge
1902	Writes to William Bateson regarding breeding experiments
1904-1910	Conducts genetics research with Bateson
1905	Publishes *Mendelism*, the first textbook on the subject
1910	Succeeds Bateson as professor of biology at Cambridge
1910	Launches the *Journal of Genetics* with Bateson
1912-1940	Named to the new professorship of genetics (formerly biology) at Cambridge
1912	Elected a Fellow of the Royal Society of London
1922	Awarded the Darwin Medal of the Royal Society of London
Jan. 3, 1967	Dies in Somerset, England

Early Life

Reginald Crundall Punnet was born on June 20, 1875 in Tonbridge, Kent, in England. He was the eldest son of a middle-class builder. At the age of nine Punnett suffered a bout of appendicitis. This event forced him to rest daily and read among his father's natural history books, thereby sparking a lifelong interest in the study of living things.

As a medical student at the University of Cambridge, Punnett excelled in the natural science tripos (honors examination), particularly in zoology.

Turning from medicine to evolutionary morphology, Punnett focused on the structure of a group of marine worms called *Nemerteans.* After several years at the University of St. Andrews, Scotland as a natural history demonstrator, Punnett returned to the University of Cambridge to become a Fellow of Caius College and later a Balfour Student in zoology.

Collaboration with Bateson

Early in the twentieth century, Gregor Mendel's nineteenth-century work found a receptive audience among many biologists, including Punnett. In 1902, Punnett wrote to the foremost British advocate of Mendel's laws, William Bateson, proposing experiments involving the inheritance of coat color. Shifting the focus of his studies, Punnett enthusiastically joined Bateson's genetics research group.

Between 1904 and 1910, Bateson and Punnett collaborated on hybridization experiments with sweet peas, domestic fowl, and other animals.

Factor Interaction

Factor interactions occur when two or more factors, inherited independently, contribute to the determination of a single physical characteristic, or phenotype.

Unit characters are ones in which genetic inheritance is determined by a single pair of factors. When they segregate, each shows complete dominance. For example, Gregor Johann Mendel used clearly segregated unit characters in pea plants such as yellow or green, smooth or wrinkled, tall or short.

Yet, this pattern is not always the case. Frequently, more than one factor is involved in the expression of a phenotype. In breeding experiments with domestic fowl, Punnett and William Bateson found that more than one factor determines the inheritance of comb shape. Certain breeds of chickens have rose, pea, or single combs. Although most crosses yield familiar Mendelian ratios, Punnett and Bateson discovered that a chicken with a rose-shaped comb bred with a chicken with a pea-shaped comb resulted in a new comb shape called walnut in all the first-generation (F1) offspring.

Explaining the appearance of walnut-shaped combs, they conjectured that the independent inheritance of two factors determined comb shape. Hence, the presence of both dominant factors, R and P, resulted in walnut combs. The presence of only the R yielded rose combs, and the presence of only the P created pea combs. Single combs resulted from the absence of both dominant factors. Furthermore, the interaction explained why crossing chickens with walnut combs yielded a 9:3:3:1 ratio, with nine walnut combs to three rose combs to three pea combs to one single combs, in the second-generation (F2) offspring (see figure).

Bibliography

Gardner, Eldon J. *Principle of Genetics.* 4th ed. New York: John Wiley & Sons, 1972.

Scott, George G. *The Science of Biology: An Introductory Study.* Rev. ed. New York: Thomas Y. Crowell, 1930.

The Second-Generation Cross of Chickens with Various Comb Shapes

Female gametes \ Male gametes	RP	Rp	rP	rp
RP	RRPP walnut	RRPp walnut	RrPP walnut	RrPp walnut
Rp	RRPp walnut	RRpp rose	RrPp walnut	Rrpp rose
rP	RrPP walnut	RrPp walnut	rrPP pea	rrPp pea
rp	RrPp walnut	Rrpp rose	rrPp pea	rrpp single

Many other types of factor interaction occur. Bateson and Punnett extended the explanatory power of Mendelism by establishing this important concept.

Confirming and extending Mendelian genetics, their research established phenomena such as factor interaction, reversion, and complementary factors. Punnett also introduced a graphical method of representing hybrid crosses, now called the Punnett square. Punnett's textbook *Mendelism* (1905) introduced the subject to a wider audience. Appearing in many editions, this popular book was translated into seven different languages.

Butterfly Mimicry and Poultry Genetics

Punnett's interests also included the investigation of butterfly mimicry, the notion of one species mimicking another for adaptive advantage. Between 1912 and 1914, he debated the University of Oxford's entomologist Edward Bagnail Poulton, a firm believer in natural selection. Opposing Poulton, Punnett insisted that mimic species emerged as a result of discontinuous mutations rather than small continuous variations. Punnett's research in this subject culminated with his work *Mimicry in Butterflies* (1915).

Encouraging practical applications of genetics, Punnett served as an expert on poultry breeding during World War I. As wartime food shortages demanded economical measures, Punnett used sex-linked plumage colors to breed chickens of different colors according to sex. With this method, the large numbers of unwanted male chicks could be detected early and destroyed. Punnett's *Heredity in Poultry* (1923) remained the standard work on poultry genetics for several decades.

Later Work

In 1910, Punnett succeeded Bateson in the newly created Cambridge chair of biology. Two years later, this position became the Arthur Balfour Chair of Genetics, the first of its kind in Great Britain. Retiring in 1940, Punnett continued research in poultry genetics into the 1950s.

Later developments in genetic theory had little impact on Punnett's consistently Mendelian outlook. Methodologically, his work illustrates part of a broader shift in biology from descriptive fieldwork to experimental laboratory research. Although best remembered for the Punnett square, he stands among a generation of scientists who established fundamental concepts in classical Mendelian genetics.

Bibliography

By Punnett

Mendelism, 1905.

Mimicry in Butterflies, 1915.

Heredity in Poultry, 1923.

About Punnett

Crew, F. A. E. "Punnett, Reginald Crundall." in *Dictionary of Scientific Biography*, edited by Charles Coulston Gillispie. Vol. 11. New York: Charles Scribner's Sons, 1970.

Crew, F. A. E. "Reginald Crundall Punnett." *Biographical Memoirs of Fellows of the Royal Society* 13 (1967).

(Robinson M. Yost)

Frederick Sanger

Disciplines: Chemistry and genetics

Contribution: Sanger was the first person to receive two Nobel Prizes in Chemistry. The first was awarded for his determination of the complete amino acid sequence of the protein insulin. Sanger's role in the development and use of a novel method to sequence deoxyribonucleic acid (DNA) resulted in a second Nobel Prize.

Aug. 13, 1918	Born in Gloucestershire, England
1939	Graduated from St. John's College, University of Cambridge
1943	Earns a Ph.D. from St. John's College
1944-1951	Awarded a medical research fellowship at Cambridge
1951	Joins the Medical Research Council
1953	Determines the entire amino acid sequence of insulin
1958	Begins work on sequence determination for DNA
1962-1983	Serves as head of the Medical Research Council Laboratory of Molecular Biology
1976	Awarded the William Hardy Prize of the Cambridge Philosophical Society
1977	Deduces the entire DNA sequence of bacterial virus Phi X 174
1977	Awarded the Copley Medal by the Royal Society of London
1980	Wins the Nobel Prize in Chemistry for his work with nucleic acids
1984	Elucidates the entire DNA sequence of the Epstein-Barr virus

Early Life

Frederick Sanger was born in Rendcombe, Gloucestershire, England, on August 13, 1918. The son of a physician, he spent his early education at Bryanston School. Sanger attended the University of Cambridge for his entire university education, earning first a B.A. in 1939 and then a doctorate in 1943 through St. John's College at the University of Cambridge. He continued his biochemistry research at Cambridge as a research fellow until 1951, at which time he joined the staff of the Medical Research Council.

Tools to Study Proteins

During the 1940s and 1950s, much chemical research focused on the hereditary molecule deoxyribonucleic acid (DNA) and proteins, the products of DNA. Sanger's primary research interest at this time was in determining the exact amino acid sequence of a protein. In the early 1940s, he experienced a significant breakthrough toward that end.

In 1945, he devised a method to use the chemical 2,4-dinitrofluorobenzene, later known as Sanger's reagent, to label one end of the protein chain. Sanger could then use acid to break up the protein into smaller fragments. Other scientists had designed a method to separate the individual amino acids from a mixture called paper chromatography.

Determining the Amino Acid Sequence of a Protein

The amino acid sequence of a protein gives vital information about its function. This sequence can be determined by the degradation and separation of the protein's components.

In order to understand the function of important proteins, it is critical to know their chemical makeup. Sanger summoned his formidable scientific skills to tackle the task of determining that makeup.

Proteins consist of subunits called amino acids, of which there are twenty different types in human beings. Sanger chose to use the protein hormone insulin, which was isolated from the pancreatic tissue of cattle, as his first subject.

Sanger had discovered a particular chemical called 2,4-dinitrofluorobenzene (later known as Sanger's reagent) that binds to one end of a chain of amino acids. Using an enzyme, a type of protein that cuts other proteins between amino acids, Sanger cut the insulin molecule into small pieces. He labeled one end with Sanger's reagent, then cut the fragments into even smaller, single amino acid pieces with the enzymes.

The individual amino acids from one labeled section were separated by a process called paper chromatography. The amino acid mixture was placed in a solvent, and the end of a strip of paper was placed in the solvent and amino acid mixture. Capillary action drew the solvent mixture up along the length of the paper, and the amino acids were separated according to their size and charge. Based on the distance of migration, the chemically labeled amino acids could be identified.

After repeating this time-consuming and tedious process hundreds of times, with long and short pieces, Sanger was able to fit together the puzzle of information into a cohesive picture that revealed the linear sequence of amino acids. It took Sanger and his collaborators eight years to map the fifty-one amino acids of insulin. The results of this monumental undertaking were published in 1953, and Sanger was awarded the Nobel Prize in Chemistry for this work in 1958.

In addition, Sanger was able to determine that there were small but significant sequence differences between insulin derived from pigs, horses, sheep, and whales. This finding had particular significance for human beings, for when human insulin was sequenced, it was found to differ slightly from that of pigs. For many years, individuals suffering from insulin-dependent diabetes had only insulin derived from pigs as a source of medicine. The systems of many individuals rejected the pig insulin because of these differences.

Sanger's methods led to the rapid sequencing of many other proteins, including enzymes of important biochemical pathways. His work paved the way for the first artificial synthesis of a protein, insulin, by 1964. His perseverance and scientific insight have led to the sequencing and synthesis of many proteins and a means to explore their functions.

Bibliography

Campbell, Neil. *Biology*. 4th ed. Redwood City, Calif.: Benjamin/Cummings, 1996.

Leone, Francis. *Genetics: The Mystery and the Promise.* Blue Ridge Summit, Pa.: McGraw-Hill, 1992.

Watson, James D. et al. *Molecular Biology of the Gene*. 4th ed. Menlo Park, Calif.: Benjamin/Cummings, 1987.

Stryer, Lubert. *Molecular Design of Life*. New York: W. H. Freeman, 1989.

Sanger planned to break down the sequence of amino acids partially, attach his reagent to one end, break these labeled fragments down to individual amino acids, and separate them using paper chromatography. In this way, he could identify which amino acid was labeled. By painstakingly repeating this procedure many times, he could generate overlapping fragments of the protein and then, as if working a jigsaw puzzle, deduce the order of the amino acids.

The Process of Sequencing DNA

Deoxyribonucleic acid (DNA) is made of a linear sequence of four different subunits called nucleotides. The sequence can be determined by complex biochemical methods.

DNA is made of repeating chemical subunits called nucleotides. The four nucleotides—adenine, cytosine, guanine, and thymine—differ by the type of organic base attached. With the advent of recombinant DNA technology in the mid-1970s, it became critical to determine the nucleotide base sequences of the DNA that makes up genes. A chemical degradation method existed soon afterward, but it was a slow process

The Four Nucleotides Found in DNA

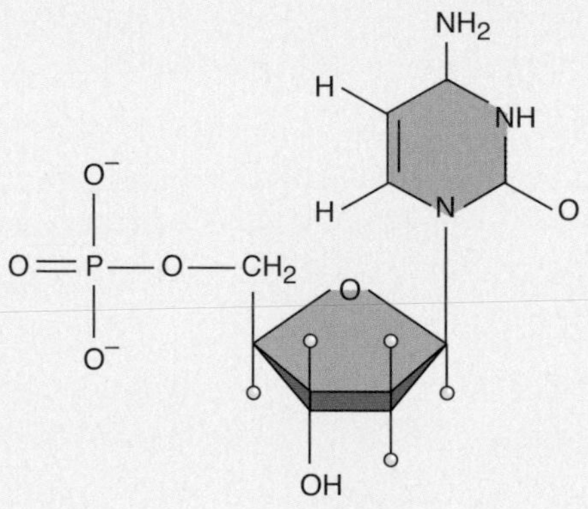

Cytosine

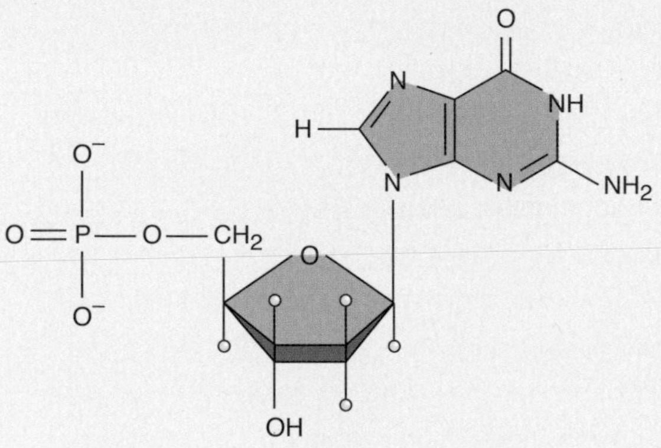

Guanine

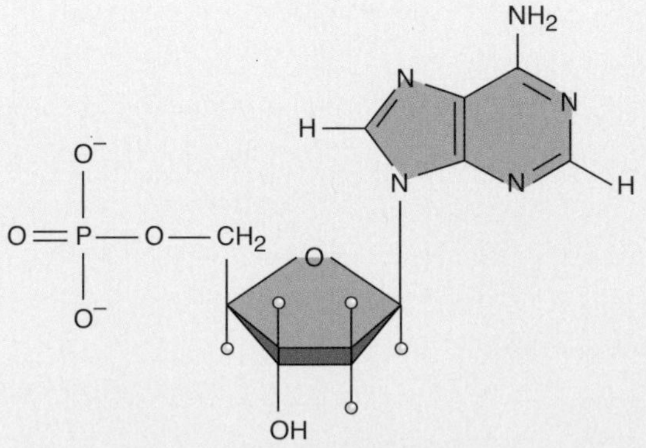

Adenine

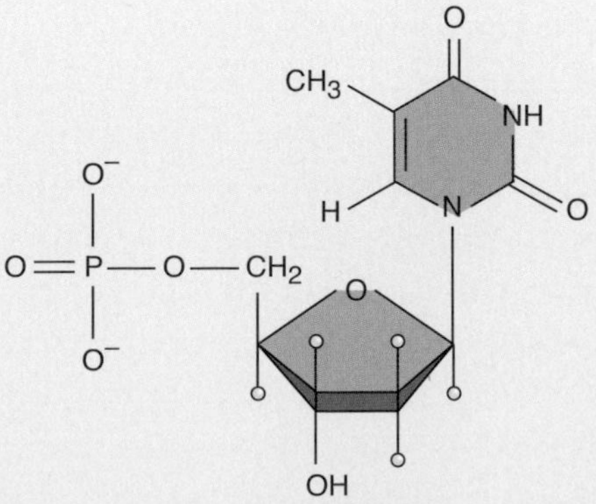

Thymine

Insulin

The protein hormone insulin had been isolated some twenty-five years earlier and was known to consist of two connected chains of fifty amino acids. Sanger chose this protein, which he obtained from cattle, for his sequence experiment.

entailing months to sequence a single gene.

Sanger and his colleagues developed a method that revolutionized DNA sequencing. In a test tube, a single strand of DNA, along with all the chemical components to synthesize a complementary strand, was mixed with a radioactively labeled nucleotide. Also included were nucleotides that would halt the DNA synthesis at one of the four types of nucleotides. After millions of molecules were replicated, the newly synthesized DNA strands were separated by gel electrophoresis. The gels were then exposed to X-ray film, which indicated the location of the radioactive tags and the lengths of DNA fragments.

Sanger's sequencing method was adapted to become automated, so that the sequence of thousands of bases could be determined in a single day. This development had a major impact on the swiftness of sequencing. It has facilitated the sequencing of the entire human genome—a formidable three billion nucleotides—through the Human Genome Project of the National Institutes of Health and the Department of Energy.

Bibliography

Nicholl, Desmond S. T. *An Introduction to Genetic Engineering*. Cambridge, England: Cambridge University Press, 1994.

Watson, James D. et al. *Molecular Biology of the Gene*. 4th ed. Menlo Park, Calif.: Benjamin/Cummings, 1987.

Stryer, Lubert. *Molecular Design of Life*. New York: W. H. Freeman, 1989.

For eight years, Sanger repeated the finely detailed, meticulous, and somewhat tedious work of the sequencing procedure. When he had deduced the sequence of many short fragments of insulin, he put together a map of how they fitted together in longer fragments and then finally the intact molecule. The results of his stunning achievement were published in 1953.

The scientific community acknowledged this major breakthrough by awarding to Sanger the Nobel Prize in Chemistry in 1958.

Sequencing Nucleic Acids

In the late 1950s, the direction of Sanger's research turned toward sequencing DNA, the chemical molecule that specifies the amino acid sequence of proteins, and ribonucleic acid (RNA), which is an intermediate between DNA and proteins. James D. Watson and Francis Crick had elucidated the three-dimensional structure of DNA in 1953 and by this time many enzymes that interact with DNA had been identified. Sanger combined these fields to develop methods to sequence nucleic acids.

Sanger first worked on RNA, which occurs in relatively short lengths. He then moved on to DNA, which can have up to 100 million base units per chain. For experimental tools, Sanger used a combination of enzymes that cut or extend DNA, radioactive labeling, and separation of DNA bases on gels, a procedure called electrophoresis.

By 1977, Sanger and his colleagues had obtained the complete sequence of the bacterial virus Phi X 174, which is composed of more than 5,400 DNA bases. Carried on by this success, they soon were able to sequence the DNA of human mitochondria (cellular organelles), which are more than 17,000 bases long, followed by the relatively huge human virus known as Epstein-Barr, with 150,000 bases.

In 1980, together with Paul Berg and Walter Gilbert, Sanger was awarded the Nobel Prize in Chemistry for his nucleic acid work. Sanger became the first person to receive two

Nobel Prizes in Chemistry and one of the elite few to receive two Nobel awards.

Legacy

The fundamental principles discovered by Sanger stimulated many areas of research. The sequences of a tremendous number of proteins and genes are now known. Many proteins essential for human life can be synthesized or produced through recombinant DNA technology. The methods that he developed greatly accelerated research and the fruits of his research will continue to have a major impact for generations to come.

Bibliography

By Sanger

"The Amino Acid Sequence in the Glycyl Chain of Insulin: The Identification of Lower Peptides from Partial Hydrolysates," *Biochemical Journal*, 1953 (with E. O. P. Thompson).

"A Rapid Method for Determining Sequences in DNA by Primed Synthesis with DNA Polymerase," *Journal of Molecular Biology*, 1975 (with A. R. Coulson).

DNA Sequencing with Chain-Terminating Inhibitors," *Proceedings of the National Academy of Sciences*, 1977 (with S. Nicklen and A. R. Coulson).

"Nucleotide Sequence of Bacteriophage γ DNA," *Journal of Molecular Biology*, 1982 (with A. R. Coulson et al.).

About Sanger

Judson, Horace Freeland. *The Eighth Day of Creation.* New York: Simon & Schuster, 1979.

Magill, Frank N., ed."Frederick Sanger." in *The Nobel Prize Winners: Chemistry.* Pasadena, Calif.: Salem Press, 1990.

Silverstein, Alvin. *Frederick Sanger: The Man Who Mapped Out a Chemical of Life.* New York: John Day, 1969.

(Karen E. Kalumuck)

George D. Snell

Disciplines: Biology, genetics, and immunology

Contribution: A pioneer in immunogenetic research, Snell discovered the major histocompatibility complex, a genetic group responsible for controlling tissue graft rejection in mice.

Dec. 19, 1903	Born in Bradford, Massachusetts
1926	Earns a B.S. in biology from Dartmouth College, New Hampshire
1930	Earns a S.D. in genetics from Harvard University
1935	Takes a position at the Jackson Laboratory in Bar Harbor, Maine
1952	Elected to the American Academy of Arts and Sciences
1962	Receives the Bertner Foundation Award
1967	Given an honorary M.D. by Charles University in Prague, Czechoslovakia
1967	Awarded the Gregor Mendel Medal of the Czechoslovak Academy of Sciences
1970	Elected to the National Academy of Sciences
1974	Awarded an honorary S.D. by Dartmouth
1976	Receives the Gairdner Foundation Award
1978	Elected a member of the French Académie des Sciences
1978	Wins the Wolf Foundation Prize in Medicine
1980	Awarded the Nobel Prize in Physiology or Medicine
June 6, 1996	Dies in Bar Harbor, Maine

Early Life

George Davis Snell, the son of an inventor and manufacturer of ignition systems for internal combustion engines, was born in 1903 and grew up in Brookline, Massachusetts.

As a boy, Snell was interested in mathematics, physics, and astronomy, but his interests were not exclusively scientific. While growing up, he also enjoyed neighborhood games of football and baseball, and, in high school he became a member of the Brookline band.

In 1926, Snell earned his B.S. in biology from Dartmouth College, New Hampshire where he was also an excellent clarinet player and Dartmouth band member. He went on to Harvard University for a doctorate in science. There, he worked with Ernest Castle, a research biologist studying Mendelian principles of genetic inheritance.

While finishing his doctoral degree, Snell became an instructor at Dartmouth College. After earning his S.D. in genetics from Harvard in 1930, he taught for a year at Brown University, Rhode Island. In 1931, he was awarded a National Research Council Fellowship and went to the University of Texas, Austin, to research the effects of X-rays on mice.

Snell's research was the first to show that X-rays cause mutations in the structure of mammalian chromosomes.

The Jackson Laboratory

Snell took a research position in 1935 at the Roscoe B. Jackson Memorial Laboratory in Bar Harbor, Maine, where he remained for the rest of his career. In his early work at the Jackson Laboratory, he continued his research on X-rays and genetic mutation in mice. Snell wanted to broaden his genetic inquiry, however, and began to conduct research into the genetic factors underlying organ and tissue transplantation. He wanted to isolate and identify the genetic loci responsible for the acceptance or rejection of grafted tissue.

In 1948, Snell and the English geneticist Peter A. Gorer, who was responsible for serologically based antigen research, reported their discovery of the H-2 locus ("H" for "histocompatibility" and "2" for "Antigen II"). This genetic site is responsible for cellular reactions that determine transplant rejection.

Further research showed that the H-2 group of linked genes is not formed at one genetic location but is made up of several different loci. Subsequently, the H-2 locus came to be known as the major histocompatibility complex (MHC). The MHC in mice controls cellular responses to grafted tissues recognized as foreign and determines successful transplantation.

Snell's research directly informed Jean Dausset's discovery of the genetically controlled histocompatibility system in humans in 1958, which led surgeons to begin performing tissue typing for organ transplants. Snell and Dausset, along with Stanley Nathenson, wrote a book called *Histocompatibility* (1976).

The Major Histocompatibility Complex

In his studies of mice, Snell discovered the major histocompatibility complex (MHC): a group of closely linked genes that determines the rejection of grafted tissue.

The first step in the discovery of the MHC was Snell's correlation of physical signs on mice, which are known as markers, to tissue graft rejection. For example, in one specially crossed strain of mice, a kinked tail was found to be a marker of subsequent tissue graft rejection.

Snell developed what are called congenic mice in order to study the function of transplantation-related genes separately. Congenic mice are identical to one another except for the specific genetic locus that is to be investigated. This method of scientific investigation, which Snell invented, allowed him to track the effects of particular genes.

Snell identified a set of approximately ten genetic loci or sites that control the antigens responsible for graft acceptance at the cellular level. An antigen is a complex molecule that initiates and mediates antibody action in the immune system. In Snell's group of sites, one locus was found to play a dominant role in controlling antigens and subsequently producing immune resistance to tissue grafts.

Peter Gorer, of Guy's Hospital in London, England, had also been working on graft rejections in specially bred strains of mice. Through his research in serology, a blood-based rather than a genetic investigation, Gorer had also discovered antigens on cell surfaces that, depending on the particular strain of mice, determined the rejection of grafted tissue. He designated these particular antigens "Antigen II." When Gorer came to work with Snell for a year at the Jackson Laboratory, they found that the genetic coding of Gorer's serology-based Antigen II was located in the identical genetic loci that Snell had isolated.

Snell's concept of histocompatibility—a term he coined in 1948—refers to the genetically programmed antigens on the cell surface that are responsible for the rejection of foreign tissue. Snell and Gorer designated the site that controlled these antigens "H-2," a combination of Snell's histocompatibility and Gorer's Antigen II. Histocompatibility antigens determine the compatibility of tissues from two different bodies.Tissues that are compatible possess similar histocompatibility antigens on the surface of their cells. Tissues that are not compatible possess different histocompatibility antigens on cellular surfaces. Matching these antigens when transplanting tissue from one body to another is necessary if the tissue is not to be attacked and, therefore, rejected by the recipient's immune system.

Snell had thought that the H-2 locus was a single gene that controlled the action of histocompatibility antigens. Further research determined that the site was a complex set of interrelated genes and was designated the major histocompatibility complex. The MHC is located in mice on chromosome number 17.

Snell's discovery of the MHC group of genes helped make possible not only human organ transplants but also research into the human immune system itself. His research laid the foundation for the study of infectious diseases and for subsequent cancer and acquired immunodeficiency syndrome (AIDS) research. Because of the far-reaching impact of Snell's pioneering work, he is considered the founder of modern immunogenetics.

Bibliography

Klein, Jan. *Biology of the Mouse Histocompatibility-2 Complex: Principles of Immunogenetics Applied to a Single System.* Berlin: Springer-Verlag, 1975.

Klein, Jan. *The Natural History of the Major Histocompatibility Complex.* New York: John Wiley & Sons, 1986.

Snell's discovery of the MHC system in mice gave the study of cancer and tumor immunology a great boost in the 1950s. The relationship between immunology and the MHC generated significant research into how immune responses might be strengthened to fight infectious diseases and cancer. Along with J. R. Tennant, Snell conducted research that linked the success of viral leukemia in certain strains of mice to the function of the histocompatibility complex.

Scientific Career and Recognition

In 1947, Snell founded the scholarly journal *Immunogenetics*, and he remained its editor until 1980. From 1957 to 1968, he was the senior staff scientist at the Jackson Laboratory. He became emeritus senior staff scientist in 1968, officially retiring in 1973.

Snell's long list of awards, prizes, and honors includes the Hektoen Silver Medal of the American Medical Association and the Career Award of the National Cancer Institute. For discovering the genetic factors that laid the groundwork for the successful transplantation of tissues and organs in humans, Snell won the 1980 Nobel Prize in Physiology or Medicine. He shared the prize with U.S. immunologist Baruj Benacerraf and French immunogeneticist Dausset.

Late in life, Snell expanded his area of inquiry once more, this time to include philosophy and ethics, publishing a book entitled *Search for a Rational Ethic* (1988). This book investigated social problems from the point of view of genetics and evolutionary theory, and it also looked at the impact of science and ethics on modern society.

In recognition of a lifetime of scientific achievement, Maine's governor Angus King signed a proclamation declaring March 14-21, 1996, as "Dr. George D. Snell Week."

Snell died on June 6, 1996.

Bibliography

By Snell

Biology of the Laboratory Mouse, 1941 (as editor).

Cell Surface Antigens: Studies in Mammals Other than Man, 1973 (with others).

Genetic and Biological Aspects of Histocompatibility Antigens, 1973 (with others).

Histocompatibility, 1976 (with Jean Dausset and Stanley Nathenson).

Search for a Rational Ethic, 1988.

About Snell

Moritz, Charles., ed. *Current Biography Yearbook 1986*. New York: H. W. Wilson, 1986.

Marx, Jean L. "1980 Nobel Prize in Physiology or Medicine." *Science* 210 (November 7, 1980).

Clark, Matt. "A Nobel Piece of Research." *Newsweek* (October 20, 1980).

Dowie, Mark. *"We Have a Donor": The Bold New World of Organ Transplants.* New York: St. Martin's Press, 1988.

(Mark Gray Henderson)

Nettie Maria Stevens

Disciplines: Biology, cell biology, and genetics
Contribution: Stevens demonstrated that sex is determined by a particular chromosome. She was the first person to establish that chromosomes exist as paired structures in body cells and the first to ascertain that certain insects have supernumerary chromosomes.

July 7, 1861	Born in Cavendish, Vermont
1880	Graduated from Westford Academy, Massachusetts
1892	Enters the Normal School in Westfield, Massachusetts
1899	Earns a B.A. from Stanford University
1900	Earns an M.A. from Stanford
1903	Earns a Ph.D. from Bryn Mawr College, Pennsylvania
1904	Named a Reader in Experimental Morphology
1905	Publishes a monograph that identifies the X and Y chromosomes
1905	Awarded the Ellen Richards Research Prize of $1,000 by the association maintaining the American Women's Table at the Naples Zoological Station
1905-1912	Awarded the rank of Associate in Experimental Morphology
1908-1909	Studies at the University of Würzburg, Germany with Theodor Boveri
May 4, 1912	Dies in Baltimore, Maryland

Early Life

Nettie Maria Stevens was the second of three children born to Ephraim and Julia Stevens. Aside from the fact that her father was a carpenter and sawyer, little is known of her family background and the first three decades of her life. She worked as a schoolteacher and a librarian for many years before continuing her education.

In September, 1892, at the age of thirty-one, Stevens entered the Normal School in Westfield, Massachusetts; she transferred as an undergraduate to Stanford University four years later. Majoring in physiology, she received her B.A. and M.A. from Stanford in 1899 and 1900, respectively.

Further Education

As an undergraduate, Stevens spent three summers at the Hopkins Seaside Laboratory in Pacific Grove, California. Her research focused on the life cycle of *Boveria*, a protozoan parasite of sea cucumbers. Her findings were published in the

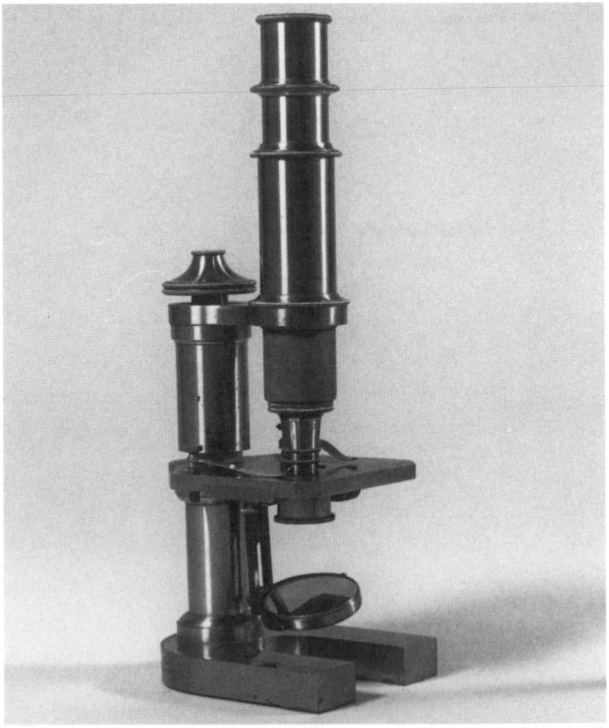

Bryn Mawr keeps the microscope Stevens used in her work in the school's Special Collections.

Proceedings of the *California Academy of Sciences* in 1901.

In 1900, Stevens entered Bryn Mawr College, Pennsylvania, as a graduate student in biology. In her second year, a fellowship enabled her to study at the Zoological Station in Naples, Italy, and at the University of Würzburg, Germany, under Theodor Boveri.

In 1903, she received a Ph.D. from Bryn Mawr with a thesis on ciliate protozoa. Stevens continued at Bryn Mawr as a research fellow in biology and an associate in experimental morphology. In 1905, the association that maintained the American Women's Table at the Naples station awarded Stevens the Ellen Richards Research Prize of $1,000, given to promote scientific research by women.

Research Interests

Stevens carried out research in three major areas of biology. Her earliest work was concerned with the morphology (physical charac teristics) and taxonomy (classification) of cibate protozoan.

The Chromosomal Determination of Sex

Stevens' most important research dealt with chromosomes and their relation to heredity.

When Stevens began her work, Gregor Johann Mendel's laws on the transmission of hereditary factors had been rediscovered in 1900, and the studies of Theodor Boveri and Walter S. Sutton on chromosome behavior had suggested that Mendel's factor might actually be associated with chromosomes. It is not known exactly when Stevens became interested in the problem of chromosomes and sex determination. In 1903, however, she described one of her research interests as the "histological side of the problems of heredity connected with Mendel's Principles of Heredity."

Stevens and Edmund Beecher Wilson worked independently to demonstrate that the sex of an organism is determined by a particular chromosome. During the period of Stevens' research, investigators were exploring the relationship between chromosomes and heredity. Although the behavior of the chromosomes had been experimentally confirmed, no trait had been traced from the chromosomes of the parent to those of the offspring, nor had a specific chromosome been linked with a specific characteristic.

Working with the mealworm (*Tenebrio molitor*) using Mendel's laws of inheritance, Stevens confirmed that males produce two kinds of sperm, one carrying a large X chromosome and the other carrying a small Y chromosome. The unfertilized eggs, however, were all alike in possessing two X chromosomes. Stevens suggested that eggs fertilized by sperm carrying X chromosomes produce females and those eggs fertilized by sperm carrying Y chromosomes produce males. Although Stevens' hypothesis was not universally accepted by biologists at the time, the theory of sex determination has now been proven and this discovery is considered to be of profound importance.

Bibliography

Wilson, Edmund B. *The Cell in Development and Heredity*. 3d ed. New York: Macmillan, 1937.

Hughes, Arthur. *A History of Cytology*. London: Abelard-Schuman, 1959.

Brush, Stephen G. "Nettie M. Stevens and the Discovery of Sex Determination by Chromosomes." *Isis* 69 (1978).

Morgan, Thomas Hunt. "The Scientific Work of Miss N. M. Stevens." *Science* 36 (1912).

Dunn, L. C. *A Short History of Genetics: The Development of Some of the Main Lines of Thought, 1864-1939*. New York: McGraw-Hill, 1965.

Later, she became interested in cytology, particularly the histology (tissue study) of regenerative processes in hydroids and planarians. In 1904, with the geneticist Thomas Hunt Morgan, she published a paper on the regenerative processes in the hydroid Tubularia.

Stevens' research was characterized by precise observations and cautious interpretations. She published thirty-eight papers in eleven years.

Stevens died of breast cancer on May 4, 1912, before she could accept the research professorship created for her by the Bryn Mawr trustees.

Bibliography

By Stevens

Studies in Spermatogenesis with Especial Reference to the "Accessory Chromosome," 1905.

"A Study of the Germ Cells of *Aphis rosae* and *Aphis oenotherae*," Journal of Experimental Zoology, 1905.

Studies in Spermatogenesis: A Comparative Study of the Heterochromosomes in Certain Species of Coleoptera, Hemiptera, and Lepidoptera, with Especial Reference to Sex Determination, 1906.

Studies on the Germ Cells of Aphids, 1906 "Further Studies on Heterochromosomes in Mosquitoes," *Biological Bulletin of the Marine Biological Laboratory*, 1911.

About Stevens

Bailey, Martha J. *American Women in Science. A Biographical Dictionary*. Santa Barbara, Calif.: ABC-CLIO, 1994.

Vare, Ethlie Ann and Greg Ptacek. *Mothers of Invention: From the Bra to the Bomb: Forgotten Women and Their Unforgettable Ideas.* New York: William Morrow, 1988.

Ogilvie, Marilyn Bailey. *Women in Science: Antiquity Through the Nineteenth Century.* Cambridge, Mass.: MIT Press, 1986.

(Margaret H. Major)

Alfred H. Sturtevant

Disciplines: Biology, genetics, and zoology

Contribution: A pioneer in classical genetics, Sturtevant discovered the principles of gene mapping, the first reparable gene defect, and the phenomenon of position effect.

Nov. 21, 1891	Born in Jacksonville, Illinois
1908	Enters Columbia University
1910	Joins the "fly room" of Thomas Hunt Morgan at Columbia University
1914	Earns a doctorate from Columbia University
1914	Remains at Columbia as a research investigator for the Carnegie Institution of Washington
1920	Discovers the first reparable gene defect, the vermillion eye color mutation in fruit flies
1925	Presents the concepts of position effect and of unequal crossing-over at meiosis
1928	Appointed a professor of genetics at the California Institute of Technology (Caltech)
1932	Travels to England and Germany as visiting professor of the Carnegie Endowment for International Peace
1951	Completes the genetic map of *Drosophila*
1968	Awarded the National Medal of Science
Apr. 5, 1970	Dies in Pasadena, California

Early Life

Alfred Henry Sturtevant, the youngest of six children, spent his early education in a one-room schoolhouse in Alabama. As a boy, one of his hobbies was drawing the genetic pedigrees of his father's horses.

In 1908, he entered Columbia University and with the encouragement of his brother, a teacher at nearby Barnard College, began reading books on heredity, thereby stimulating his interest in genetics.

Sturtevant submitted his findings on coat color inheritance patterns in horses to the noted Columbia University geneticist Thomas Hunt Morgan. Morgan encouraged Sturtevant to publish his findings, which appeared in the *Biological Bulletin* in 1910, and invited him to join his research group.

The "Fly Room"

Morgan's cramped laboratory in which as many as eight scientists worked at one time was called the "fly room." In this rarified atmosphere of excited exchange and debate of scientific ideas, Sturtevant worked with Morgan, H. J. Muller, and C. B. Bridges, among others. While still an undergraduate student, Sturtevant developed the first chromosome map of *Drosophila melanogaster*, the fruit fly, and introduced the concept of using the frequency of crossing-over of linked genes as a means to construct such a genetic map.

Sturtevant's doctoral work was completed in 1914, and he remained at Columbia in the "fly room" conducting research until 1928. During this time, Sturtevant published works that significantly advanced the field of genetics, including a 1925 paper entitled "The Effects of Unequal Crossing Over at the Bar Locus in *Drosophila*," which detailed the phenomena of unequal crossing-over of chromosomes during meiosis and of position effect in the expression of genes. Additional publications described the maternal inheritance pattern of some genetic traits, including shell coiling in snails.

Sturtevant published numerous papers on his genetic research on fruit flies.

The California Institute of Technology

In 1928, Sturtevant became professor of genetics in the new division of biology established by Morgan at the California Institute of Technology (Caltech) in Pasadena. Sturtevant maintained an active laboratory in the style of the "fly room." In addition, he collaborated extensively with his colleagues in genetics and taught courses in genetics, general biology, and entomology.

Sturtevant combined his expertise as a naturalist with his skills as a geneticist to pursue evolutionary studies of several *Drosophila* species, and, in 1935, he published a series of three "Essays on Evolution" in the *Quarterly Review of Biology*. He also was able to complete the difficult task of elucidating a genetic map of the last, tiny fourth chromosome of *Drosophila*.

After 1951, Sturtevant also published articles on the genetic effects of high-energy radiation on humans and the social implications of human genetics.

In his 1954 presidential address to the Pacific Division of the American Association for the Advancement of Science, Sturtevant warned of the genetic hazards of fallout from the testing of atomic bombs.

Sturtevant remained at Caltech pursuing an active research program until his death in 1970. His last published work, *A History of Genetics* (1965) was an outgrowth of his lectures at many universities and a lifelong interest in the history of science.

Bibliography

By Sturtevant

The Mechanism of Mendelian Heredity, 1915 (with T. H. Morgan, H. J. Muller, and C. B. Bridges).

The North American Species of Drosophila, 1921.

An Introduction to Genetics, 1939 (with G. W. Beadle).

Lewis, E. B., ed. *Genetics and Evolution, Selected Papers of A. H. Sturtevant*, 1961.

A History of Genetics, 1965.

About Sturtevant

McMurray, Emily J., ed. "A. H. Sturtevant." *in Notable Twentieth-Century Scientists*, Detroit, Mich.: Gale Research, 1995.

Emerson, Sterling. "Alfred Henry Sturtevant." *Annual Review of Genetics* 5 (1971).

(Karen E. Kalumuck)

Gene Mapping in Chromosomes

The relative distance between genes linked to the same chromosome can be determined by the frequency of crossing-over between genes.

Sturtevant observed that on occasion the offspring of a genetic cross exhibit combinations of traits unlike those of either parent. He mated fruit flies with two or more particular traits known to be located on the same chromosome—one homozygous recessive for both traits and the other heterozygous for both—and counted the percentage of progeny exhibiting new combinations of traits, called recombinants.

Sturtevant determined that the exchange of chromosome pieces between a homologous pair of chromosomes of a heterozygote during the process of meiosis, or crossing-over, resulted in the recombination of traits. For example, if one parent fly was purple-eyed and short-winged, and the other parent was red-eyed and long-winged, all progeny should have resembled one of the parents. A small percentage of offspring, however, were always purple-eyed and long-winged, or red-eyed and short-winged because of crossing-over in the heterozygous parent. In addition, Sturtevant discovered that the farther apart the two genes are on a chromosome, the more frequently they will cross-over, resulting in more recombinant offspring.

Armed with this information and performing many genetic crosses, he was able to elucidate linear maps of the chromosomal location of genes and to infer the distances between them.

Sturtevant's research led to the production of genetic maps for a variety of organisms and was a major advance in the understanding of how the genetic material is organized in all organisms, including humans.

Bibliography

Gronick, Larry and Mark Wheelis. *The Cartoon Guide to Genetics*. New York: Harper and Row, 1994.

Suzuki, David et al. *An Introduction to Genetic Analysis*. New York: W. H. Freeman, 1989.

Jacob, François. *The Logic of Life: A History of Heredity*. New York: Pantheon Books, 1974.

Jack William Szostak

Areas of Achievement: Biology and genetics

Contributions: Szostak created the world's first yeast artificial chromosome. His research led to scientists being able to locate genes in mammals, allowing for gene manipulation. He has also done research in establishing the relationship between simple chemicals and how they can emerge into primitive cells by building an early cell in a test tube.

Nov. 9, 1952	Born in London, England
1968	Begins undergraduate studies at McGill University, Montreal
1970	Receives B.S. in cell biotics at McGill
1977	Earns Ph.D. in biochemistry at Cornell University, New York
1984	Joins Massachusetts General Hospital and the Department of Molecular Biology
1988	Begins tenured professorship at Harvard Medical School
1994	Awarded the National Academy of Sciences Award in Molecular Biology
1997	Awarded the Sigrist Prize
1998	Elected to the National Academy of Sciences
2000	Awarded the Medal of the Genetics Society of America
2006	Receives the Mary Woodard Lasker Award and Benjamin Franklin Medal
2009	Wins the Nobel Prize in Physiology or Medicine

Early Life

Born in London during the great fog of 1952, Szostak was the son of a Royal Canadian Air Force pilot. The family was living in England while Szostak's father was being trained in aeronautical engineering at Imperial College, London. The following year, the Szostaks went back to Ottawa. The family would continue to move among different air force bases in Germany, Montreal, and Ottawa, depending on his father's appointments.

Szostak lived the charmed childhood of a science enthusiast: his father built him a chemistry lab and through her job at a chemical-testing laboratory, his mother provided "remarkably dangerous" chemicals he needed to experiment beyond the scope of store-bought chemistry sets.

When he looks back on his childhood, Szostak says his fondest memories are of learning about fractions, discovering quadratic equations in 5th grade, and landing his first summer job at the chemical-testing laboratory where his mother worked. At home in the basement chemistry lab, he also remembers the glass tube that got embedded in a wooden ceiling rafter, the result of an explosion that erupted when he failed to carefully separate the hydrogen evolved during electrolysis from ambient air.

Szostak graduated from Riverdale High School in Quebec, inspired to study biology. By age 15, Jack William Szostak was on his way to college and an outstanding career in molecular biology.

In 1970, he received a bachelor of science degree in cell biology at the age of 17. Although his age difference sometimes created socially awkward situations, being promoted quickly was more desirable to Szostak than remaining in classes that did not challenge him.

After completing his Ph.D. in biochemistry at Cornell University, New York, in 1977, Szostak moved to Harvard Medical School to start his own laboratory at the Sydney Farber Cancer Institute.

The Origins of Life

Szostak's long-term effort is to decipher how life arose on Earth. He hopes to answer fundamental questions about evolution's earliest steps. Szostak and his team are interested in the transition from chemistry to early biology on early Earth.

In a scenario that Szostak says took place about 500 million years ago, the right chemistry occurred that could make building blocks of life happen: the right molecules sparked life. Szostak and his colleagues want to determine how, and hope examine Darwinian evolution taking place in its earliest stages.

In Vitro Selection

Szostak created and developed a technique called in vitro selection, which is used to study the evolution of biological molecules. The process involves screening large numbers of molecules for forms that have a particular function.

Szostak and his colleagues evolved RNAs that bind to ATP, a common biological substrate, from a massive library of 1,000 trillion random RNA sequences. Artificially evolved RNAs that bind to target molecules are now known as aptamers. Szostak's team also used in vitro selection to evolve catalytic RNAs, called ribozymes, from trillions of random-sequence RNA molecules. Ribozymes are RNA molecules that can catalyze chemical reactions similar to protein enzymes. The goal was to create an RNA molecule that catalyzes its own replication. An RNA molecule able to do that would be a prime early candidate for life. Szostak's team created diverse molecules that look much like RNA or DNA but don't exist in nature.

Szostak is currently investigating in vitro selection for its ability to identify small molecules that bind specific target proteins. If successful, the technique may provide a streamlined way to pinpoint potentially useful drugs to fight disease.

Bibliography

"The Origins of Cellular Life," Our Scientists, Howard Hughes Medical Institute, May 30, 2012, http://www.hhmi.org/scientists/jack-w-szostak

"HHMI Researcher Jack Szostak Wins 2009 Nobel Prize in Physiology or Medicine," Howard Hughes Medical Institute, http://www.hhmi.org/news/hhmi-researcher-jack-szostak-wins-2009-nobel-prize-physiology-or-medicine, October 5, 2009

Bibliography

By Szostak

"Yeast transformation: a model system for the study of recombination," *Proceedings of the National Academy of Sciences*, USA, 78:6354–6358, 1981 (with T. L. Orr-Weaver and R. J. Rothstein).

"The double-strand-break repair model for recombination," *Cell*, 33:25–35: (1983) (with T. L. Orr-Weaver, R. J. Rothstein and F. Stahl).

"A mutant with a defect in telomere elongation leads to senescence in yeast," *Cell* 57, 633–643, (1989) (with V. Lundblad).

"In vitro selection of RNA molecules that bind specific ligands," *Nature* 346, 818–822 (1990) (with A. E. Ellington).

Synthesizing life," *Nature*, 409:387–390, (2001) (with D. P. Bartel and P. L. Luis).

"Origins of life: Systems chemistry on early Earth," *Nature*; 459 (7244):171-2, (May 14, 2009).

"Attempts to define life do not help to understand the origin of life," *Journal of Biomolecular Structure and Dynamics*, 29 (4): 599-600: (2012).

"The eightfold path to non-enzymatic RNA replication," *Journal of Systems Chemistry* 3:2, (2012).

About Szostak

"Life's Beginnings: Studying how life bloomed on Earth—and might emerge elsewhere," Harvard Magazine, September-October, 2013, http://harvardmagazine.com/2013/09/life-s-beginnings

"The 2009 Nobel Prize in Physiology or Medicine—Press Release". Nobelprize.org. Nobel Media AB 2013. Web. 24 Sep 2013. http://www.nobelprize.org/nobel_prizes/medicine/laureates/2009/press.html

(Tsitsi D. Wakhisi)

Hugo de Vries

Disciplines: Botany and genetics

Contribution: De Vries rediscovered Gregor Johann Mendel's laws of heredity. He advanced the idea that mutations are the chief source of genetic variation and the major method by which new species formed.

Feb. 16, 1848	Born at Haarlem, the Netherlands
1870	Studies with Wilhelm Hofmeister in Heidelberg, Germany
1871	Works in Julius von Sachs' laboratory in Würzburg, Germany
1877	Earns a Ph.D. in plant physiology
1878-1918	Serves as a professor of botany at the University of Amsterdam
1889	Publishes *Intracellulare Pangenesis* (*Intracellular Pangenesis*, 1910), marking the beginning of his work in heredity and variation
1901-1903	Publishes *Die Mutationstheorie* (*The Mutation Theory*, 1909-1910), which describes Mendel's laws of heredity and his discovery of mutation
1905	Publishes Species and Varieties
1906	Awarded the Darwin Medal for his work in genetics and evolution
1907	Publishes *Plant Breeding*, dealing with his work in plant heredity
1918	Retires from Amsterdam and settles in Lunteren, the Netherlands
1928-1929	Awarded a gold medal by the Linnean Society for his contributions to botany
May 21, 1935	Dies in Lunteren

Early Life

Hugo Marie de Vries (pronounced "duh vrees"), the son of Gerrit, a government official, and Maria, the daughter of a professor in archaeology at Leiden University, grew up in Haarlem, the Netherlands, an area marked by beautiful vegetation. He developed his love for plants from these surroundings. When his family moved to The Hague in 1862, Hugo attended the Gymnasium (high school) there.

When de Vries began his studies at Leiden University, the Netherlands, he was already quite knowledgeable in botany because of his early interest in plants.

After completing his undergraduate work, he went to the University of Heidelberg to study plant physiology with Professor Wilhelm Hofmeister.

Later, he worked in the laboratory of Julius von Sachs in Würzburg, Germany. He received his doctorate in 1877 with a dissertation on the "stretching" of cells as a result of osmosis.

Teaching and Research

De Vries began teaching as a lecturer at the newly formed University of Amsterdam and then became instructor and eventually professor of plant physiology He continued his studies on the passage of water into and out of the cell (osmosis) and the laws governing this process.

He discovered that when cells are placed in solutions that have the same amount of dissolved substances (solutes), there is no net loss or gain of water. In other words, its isotonic point is reached.

Work in Heredity and Evolution

After working on the physiology of plants, de Vries turned to experiments on plant heredity inspired by Charles Darwin's evolutionary theory. De Vries' book *Intracellulare Pangenesis* (1889; *Intracellular Pangenesis*, 1910) further developed Darwin's theory of heredity—pangenesis—but did not include the notion that environmentally induced traits could be inherited. He proposed that discrete (separate) particles carried hereditary information.

De Vries repeated Gregor Johann Mendel's classic experiments, leading to the rediscovery of Mendel's principles of heredity—segregation and dominance. This work reinforced the idea that the hereditary units are discrete units.

De Vries continued his work in plant genetics and used his findings to advance his own model of evolution. He claimed that variation in nature was caused primarily by mutation of the genetic characters. He defined mutations as sudden, large, and discrete changes in hereditary factors. He reasoned that evolution consists of rare but drastic changes, while Darwin and his successors contended that evolution resulted from gradual shifts of species over generations.

De Vries devoted the rest of his life to research in evolution, publishing more than 700 books and papers. After he retired, he lived in Lunteren, the Netherlands, where he continued his experiments with plants in his extensive garden until his death in 1935. After de Vries' death, his theory of evolution was supported by only a few geneticists, but his concept of gene mutation became an important part of genetic theory.

Bibliography

By de Vries

Intracellulare Pangenesis, 1889 (*Intracellular Pangenesis*, 1910).

Die Mutationstheorie: Versuche und Beobachtungen über die Entstehung von Arten im Pflanzenreich, 1901-1903 (2 vols.; *The Mutation Theory: Experiments and Observations on the Origin of Species in the Vegetable Kingdom*, 1909-1910, 2 vols.).

Species and Varieties: Their Origin by Mutation, 1905.

Plant Breeding: Comments on the Experiments of Nilsson and Burbank, 1907.

About de Vries

Cleland, R. "Hugo de Vries." *Proceedings of The American Philosophical Society* 76 (1936).

Allen, Garland E. "Hugo de Vries and the Reception of the 'Mutation Theory'." *Journal of the History of Biology* 2 (1969).

Blakeslee, Alfred F. "The Work of Hugo de Vries." *Scientific Monthly* 36 (1933).

(Joel S. Schwartz)

De Vries' Discovery of Mutation and Evolution Theory

De Vries' concept that the discrete factors responsible for genetic traits could undergo sudden and radical change remains an important part of genetic theory.

De Vries discovered mutations by studying the different varieties of *Oenothera lamarckiana* (evening primrose). He reasoned that variation was the result of abrupt changes in the genetic factors (pangenes). He took the name "pangene" from Charles Darwin's theory of pangenesis, and it was later shortened to "gene." De Vries called the radical changes "mutations."

He postulated that plants formed by mutations were different enough from their parents to be considered a new species. The short period of time that plants could produce mutants was referred to as the mutation period. De Vries called useful mutations "progressive" and those that were useless or harmful "retrogressive." He believed that only progressive mutations could lead to the formation of new species.

Mutations account for some of the variation in nature, but not to the extent that de Vries suggested. Later experiments performed with evening primrose by other scientists showed that the "mutations" observed by de Vries were mainly the result of other causes; actual mutation was responsible for only a few radical changes.

Bibliography

Mayr, Ernst. *The Growth of Biological Thought: Diversity, Evolution, and Inheritance.* Cambridge, Mass.: The Belknap Press of Harvard University Press, 1987.

Dodson, E. O. "Mendel and the Rediscovery of His Work." *Scientific Monthly* 58 (1955).

Dunn, L. C. *A Short History of Genetics.* New York: McGraw-Hill, 1965.

James D. Watson

Disciplines: Biology, cell biology, and genetics
Contribution: Watson was the codiscoverer of the structure of deoxyribonucleic acid (DNA). For this work, he was awarded the Nobel Prize in Physiology or Medicine in 1962.

Apr. 6, 1928	Born in Chicago, Illinois
1950	Awarded a Ph.D. in zoology from Indiana University
1950-1951	Conducts research as a National Research Council Fellow at the University of Copenhagen, Denmark
1951	Joins the Cavendish Laboratory at the University of Cambridge, England
1953	Appointed senior research fellow in biology at the California Institute of Technology (Caltech)
1955	Returns to the Cavendish Laboratory to collaborate with Crick
1956	Joins the faculty of Harvard University
1962	Awarded the Nobel Prize in Physiology or Medicine
1962	Elected to the National Academy of Sciences
1968	Takes over as director of Cold Spring Harbor Laboratories
1977	Awarded the Presidential Medal of Freedom
1988-1992	Serves as associate director and then director of the National Center for Human Genome Research

Early Life

James Dewey Watson was born in Chicago in 1928, where he attended public schools. He enrolled at the University of Chicago when he was fifteen years old and received a B.S. in zoology in 1947. Watson pursued graduate studies at Indiana University, where he studied the effects of radiation of bacterial virus multiplication. He was awarded a doctoral degree for this work in 1950. During his graduate studies, he was deeply influenced by the geneticists Hermann Joseph Muller and T. M. Sonneborn, and the microbiologist Salvador Edward Luria, who directed his thesis work.

An Interest in DNA

After completing his Ph.D., Watson continued his studies of bacterial viruses as a National Research Council Fellow at the University of Copenhagen. During a trip to Italy in 1951 he met Maurice H. F. Wilkins and saw the X-ray diffraction pattern of crystalline deoxyribonucleic acid (DNA).

The Three-Dimensional Structure of DNA

Deoxyribonucleic acid (DNA) is a double helical molecule with alternating sugars and phosphates on the outside and paired bases on the inside.

For years, many scientists worked intensely to discover the structure of DNA, the chemical molecule that controls heredity. Several pieces of the puzzle existed, but it was not until Watson began collaborative research with Francis Crick that the puzzle was put together and the structure of DNA was described.

It was known that DNA consists of sugar molecules, phosphate molecules, and four different organic bases called adenine, thymine, guanine, and uracil. Erwin Chargaff had determined that DNA molecules always contain equal amounts of adenine and thymine and equal amounts of guanine and cytosine.

The biochemist Maurice H. F. Wilkins had isolated pure DNA fibers that chemist Rosalind E. Franklin used to take excellent X-ray diffraction photographs. These photographs gave a suggestion as to the three-dimensional shape of the DNA molecule. Wilkins showed Franklin's X-ray diffraction photographs to Watson and Crick, without asking her permission. The photographs suggested to Watson and Crick a way that all the DNA components would fit together.

They built huge molecular models until one fitted the X-ray pattern shown by the photograph. The DNA molecule is a double helix, like a twisted ladder, with the sugars and phosphates alternating to form the sides of the ladder and the bases paired in the center forming the rungs of the ladder. Adenine always pairs with thymine, and guanine with cytosine, which accounts for the equal amount of the chemicals as determined by Chargaff.

It was known that DNA replicates itself every time that a cell divides. Since the DNA bases are held together in the center by weak hydrogen bonds, Watson and Crick hypothesized that the molecule could easily unzip into two pieces. Each half could then serve as a template for free nucleotides (the base, sugar, and phosphate subunits of DNA) to make a complementary strand. Other scientists later proved this hypothesis to be correct through extensive experimentation.

Elucidation of the double helical structure of DNA set the stage for future scientists to determine the nature of how this molecule self-replicates, how the sequence of bases encodes hereditary information, and how the information in genes is converted into proteins. Since all living organisms possess DNA, this information served to unlock the genetic secrets of all organisms on Earth and paved the way for the revolution in recombinant DNA technology that has had, and will continue to have, massive scientific, medical, social, and ethical implications for all of humankind.

Bibliography

Watson, James D. *The Double Helix*. New York: Atheneum, 1968.

Judson, H. F. *The Eighth Day of Creation: Makers of the Revolution in Biology*. New York: Simon & Schuster, 1979.

Asimov, Isaac. *How Did We Find Out About DNA?* New York: Walker, 1985.

Pollack, Robert *Signs of Life: The Language and Meanings of DNA*. Boston, Mass.: Houghton Mifflin, 1994.

This encounter was a significant force in turning Watson's research interests to the chemical structure of DNA and proteins.

In 1951, Watson received an appointment to the Cavendish Laboratory in Cambridge, England, where he met Francis Crick. Crick was also interested in deciphering the structure of DNA, and they became close collaborators. Many scientists around the world were trying to unlock the secrets of DNA's structure. This piece of information was regarded as the holy grail of biochemical research, and the competition to be the first to describe the structure of DNA was intense.

Elucidating the Structure

By studying the X-ray diffraction patterns of DNA, Wilkins was able to determine that DNA has a double helical structure. Rosalind E. Franklin added another important piece of information: The phosphate groups are situated on the outside of the helix.

Using this information and that of other researchers, Watson and Crick postulated that DNA is a double helix, consisting of two parallel chains of alternating sugar and phosphate groups on the outside of the helix and patterns of four different organic bases bound together in the center of the molecule, like the rungs of a ladder.

They constructed a variety of molecular models of DNA until one provided an identical pattern to the X-ray diffraction patterns seen by Wilkins and Franklin. Their results were published in the scientific journal *Nature* in March, 1953. They had won the race for the structure.

Beyond the Structure of DNA

Watson continued to pursue research in the genetic code at the California Institute of Technology (Caltech) from 1953 to 1955 and again with Crick at the Cavendish Laboratory from 1955 to 1956. He accepted a faculty position at Harvard University in 1956. During this time, his research interests focused on the role of ribonucleic acid (RNA) in protein synthesis.

The significance of the discovery of DNA was recognized by the world, and, in 1962 Watson, Crick, and Wilkins were awarded the Nobel Prize in Physiology or Medicine for their pioneering DNA research.

Elucidating the structure of DNA was one of the seminal discoveries of the twentieth century. It opened the doors to advances in recombinant DNA technology, human genetics research, and a fundamental understanding of the molecular mechanisms of heredity.

Cold Spring Harbor Laboratory

Watson became the director of Cold Spring Harbor Laboratory, New York, in 1968. His research focus expanded to meld his passion for the nucleic acids with his earlier love of virology. Much of his research in later years focused on the induction of cancer by viruses.

The Human Genome Project

In the late 1980s, the U.S. government began to finance the Human Genome Project, a major effort involving hundreds of laboratories, the goal of which was to determine the entire DNA sequence found in human beings. Through this information, it was believed that, among other possibilities, human genes could be mapped and disease-causing genes could be localized, tested for, and possibly corrected.

The National Center for Human Genome Research, a division of the National Institutes of Health, was created to oversee the Human Genome Project. Watson was appointed associate director of the center from 1988 to 1989, then director from 1989 to 1992. In addition to supporting the scientific research involved with the project, he was a strong proponent of examining the ethical issues surrounding the ability to map and sequence the human genome.

Bibliography

By Watson

"Molecular Structure of Nucleic Acids: A Structure for Deoxyribose Nucleic Acid" in *Nature*, 1953 (with Francis Crick).

"Physical Studies on Ribonucleic Acid," *Nature*, 1954.

Molecular Biology of the Gene, 1965.

The Double Helix: A Personal Account of the Discovery of DNA, 1968.

The DNA Story: A Documentary History of Gene Cloning, 1981 (with John Tooze).

Molecular Biology of the Cell, 1983 (with Bruce Alberts et al.).

Recombinant DNA: A Short Course, 1983 (with Tooze and David Kurtz).

Molecular Biology of the Gene, rev. ed, 1987 (with Nancy H. Hopkins et al.).

The Human Genome Project: Past, Present, and Future, 1990.

Houses for Science: A Pictorial History of Cold Spring Harbor Laboratory, with Landmarks of Twentieth Century Genetics: A Series of Essays, 1991 (with Elizabeth L. Watson).

About Watson

Baldwin, Joyce. *DNA Pioneer: James Watson and the Double Helix*. New York: Walker, 1994.

Newton, David E. *James Watson and Francis Crick: Discovery of the Double Helix and Beyond*. New York: Facts on File, 1992.

Olby, Robert C. *The Path to the Double Helix*. Seattle, Wash.: University of Washington Press, 1974.

(Karen E. Kalumuck)

Robert Allan Weinberg

Areas of Achievement: Genetics and biology

Contribution: Weinberg discovered the first human cancer-causing gene and the first tumor suppressor gene, the Rb gene.

Nov. 11, 1942	Born in Pittsburgh, Pennsylvania
1964	Receives B.S. at Massachusetts Institute of Technology (MIT)
1969	Receives Ph.D. in biology at MIT
1982	Helps found the Whitehead Institute
1984	Receives the Bristol-Myers Award for Distinguished Achievement in Cancer Research
1985	Elected to the National Academy of Sciences
1987	Receives the Alfred P. Sloan, Jr., Prize
1989	Elected to the American Academy of Arts and Sciences
1992	Elected to the Royal Swedish Academy of Sciences
1997	Receives the National Science Foundation's National Medal of Science
2000	Elected to the Institute of Medicine
2004	Receives the Wolf Prize in Medicine
2006	Receives the Landon-American Association for Cancer Research (AACR) Prize
2013	Awarded the $3 million Inaugural Breakthrough Prize in Life Sciences

Early Life

The son of German immigrants, Robert Weinberg grew up in Pittsburgh, and learned to speak German at home. He was always curious about how things worked. As a child he would take apart electric trains to see how they operated.

Weinberg chose the Massachusetts Institute of Technology (MIT) for his undergraduate and graduate studies because his parents' friends had gone there. He pursued medicine, he said, because "in those days, young Jewish boys became doctors." He later switched to biology when he realized that doctors did not get much sleep at night.

His transition from medicine to biology was a rocky one. Weinberg received a "D" in introductory biology at MIT. However, by his junior year, Weinberg was interested in the new discoveries in microbiology. The genetic code was being deciphered, and molecular biology fascinated him.

Outside of his studies, another movement fascinated him—the civil rights era. A year into his Ph.D. studies at MIT, Weinberg put his studies on hold. He left MIT in 1965 to teach at Stillman College, a predominantly black institution in Tuscaloosa, Alabama, where the fight for desegregation was dominating national headlines. He led the school's undergraduate biology department during the week, but on weekends he was helping Greene County sharecroppers who had been evicted from their land because they had registered to vote. He paid for and delivered sacks of flour and rice and beans to the displaced families.

He returned to MIT the following year and earned his Ph.D. in 1969. Weinberg also completed two postdoctoral fellowships at the Weizmann Institute of Science in Rehovot in Israel, and at the Salk Institute for Biological Studies, in La Jolla, California, where he worked with the DNA tumor virus SV40 to study RNA metabolism.

The Hallmarks of Cancer

In 2000, Weinberg shared his comprehensive insights into what makes cancer cells abnormal by cowriting with Douglas Hanahan the seminal paper, "Hallmarks of Cancer." The paper covered six principles of the differences between normal and cancer cells.

In their follow-up paper in 2011, "Hallmarks of Cancer: The Next Generation," the authors cited two "emerging hallmarks" that future research may show to be crucial to malignancy–the ability of an aberrant cell to reprogram its metabolism to feed its wildfire growth and to evade destruction by the immune system.

Weinberg has published five books, among them two editions of a textbook, *The Biology of Cancer*, which is used widely to describe the findings of modern cancer research over the past four decades.

Weinberg is the director of the Ludwig Center for Molecular Oncology at MIT, where he is also a professor of biology and a legend in the field of cancer research.

Bibliography

By Weinberg

"Mechanism of Activation of a Human Oncogene," *Nature*, Nov. 11, 1982.

"The Biology of Cancer," *Garland Science Textbooks*, 2nd Edition, June 2006, 2013.

"One Renegade Cell," *Science Masters*, October 1, 1999.

"Racing to the Beginning of the Road: The Search for the Origin of Cancer," *Harmony Books*, May 1996.

"Genes and the Biology of Cancer," *Scientific American Library*, October 1992 (with Harold Varmus).

"Oncogenes and the Molecular Origins of Cancer," *Monograph Series* No. 18, March 1, 1990, Cold Spring Harbor (as editor).

"Creation of Human Tumor Cells with Defined Genetic Elements," *Nature*, 1999.

About Weinberg

Lowry, Fran. "Robert Weinberg Rewarded for Oncogene Discovery, Recipient of the 2011 ASCO Science of Oncology Award," *MedScape Multi Specialty*, http://www.medscape.com/viewarticle/742131, May 5, 2011.

Fand, Beth. "Those Eureka Moments Glisten: A Conversation With Robert A. Weinberg, Ph.D.," Incollingo, http://www.onclive.com/publications/oncology-live/2011/july-2011/those-eureka-moments-glisten-a-conversation-with-robert-a-weinberg-phd, ONC Live, 2011.

(Tsitsi D. Wakhisi)

Unraveling the Mystery of Cancer

Among Weinberg's earliest achievements was establishing that individual cancer-causing genes—oncogenes—cause cancer. Medical researchers previously had thought cancer was caused by chemical carcinogens, tumor viruses and radiation. Weinberg's laboratory was the first to show that an activated human gene (ras) could, by itself, cause tumors when introduced into noncancerous cells.

In 1977, he and his colleagues began studying viral oncogenes, which led to the 1979 discovery of the first cellular oncogene in mammalian cells. The team produced tumors in healthy mice by transferring oncogenes to normal cells. Weinberg used new forms of genetic engineering to isolate genes in the cells of human tumors. He showed that these oncogenes, when introduced into normal mouse cells grown in a laboratory environment, modified the normal cells and made them cancerous. The experiment involved taking genes from cells that had been exposed to a chemical carcinogen and putting those genes into normal cells. The result was that the normal cells became cancerous, proving for the first time that cancer is a genetic disease.

In 1986, Weinberg and his colleagues isolated the first tumor suppressor gene, the retinoblastoma gene. These achievements revolutionized the way scientists think about the origins of human cancer and led in 1999 to their creation of the first genetically defined human cancer cell.

Bibliography

Angier, Natalie and Lewis Thomas. *Natural Obsessions: The Search for the Oncogene.* Boston, Mass.: Houghton Mifflin, 1988.

Johnson, George. "Cancer's Secrets Come Into Sharper Focus," *New York Times*, Aug. 15, 2011.

Nancy Sabin Wexler

Areas of Achievement: Genetics, psychology, and health administration

Contribution: Wexler discovered the location of the gene that causes Huntington's disease (Huntington's chorea) and created a chromosomal test to identify sufferers

July 19, 1945	Born in Washington, D.C.
1969	Co-founds the Michigan Chapter of the Committee to combat Huntington's Disease
1974	Earns a Ph.D. in clinical psychology
1976	Becomes executive director of the Congressional Commission for the Control of Huntington's Disease and its Consequences
1979	Appointed to the Commission for the Control of Huntington's Disease
1983	Named president of the Hereditary Disease Foundation
1985	Becomes associate professor, clinical neuropsychology, Columbia University
1987	Appointed to the Advisory Panel on Mapping the Human Genome
1990	Becomes a fellow at the Hastings Center
1993	Becomes Higgins Professor of Neuropsychology, Columbia University
1998	Named Fellow of New York Academy of Sciences
2007	Receives the Mary Woodard Lasker Award for Public Service

Early Life

Nancy Wexler was born in the nation's capital, Washington, DC, but she and her sister, Alice, grew up in Topeka, Kansas. Their mother, Leonore Wexler, a geneticist, and their father, Dr. Milton Wexler, a psychoanalyst and clinical psychologist, exposed the girls to different areas of science, including the environment, nature, physics, and astronomy.

A Family Affair

Wexler and her sister are the daughters, granddaughters and nieces of Huntington's disease sufferers. Their grandfather died from the illness as did their mother and her three brothers.

The fatal, neurological and genetic disorder called Huntington's disease is inherited. Each child of a parent with the disease has a 50-50 chance of inheriting it. It usually strikes adults between the ages of 35 and 45. As a slowly progressive disease, Huntington's can last anywhere from

10 to 25 years. The most damaging changes usually occur early in the disease so that people lose the capacity to work or head a household. For example, Wexler's mother's symptoms progressed from her fingers moving constantly to uncontrollable motions. "When she sat, her spasmodic body movements would propel her chair along the floor until it reached a wall, her head would bang repeatedly against the wall. To keep her from hurting herself at night, her bed was padded with lamb's wool," Wexler said.

In 1968, after his wife was diagnosed as having Huntington's disease, Milton Wexler started the Hereditary Disease Foundation, which introduced his two daughters to scientists, geneticists and molecular biologists.

Wexler was greatly motivated by her family to investigate Huntington's disease. In 1969, she coorganized the Michigan Chapter of the Committee to Combat Huntington's Disease to spread understanding and support to families affected by Huntington's Disease.

Huntington's Disease, the Chromosome Key

With a family history of Huntington disease, Wexler thought at an early age she would want to know as much as possible about the disease. She attended several workshops.

In 1972, Wexler learned about the work of Dr. Americo Negrette, a Venezuelan physician who had identified the disease in small villages along the shores of Lake Maracaibo, Venezuela, in 1955. He searched world literature to identify the illness that caused the villagers to have abnormal "dance-like" movements. He discovered they suffered from Huntington's, the disease named after physician George Huntington, who first described the illness in 1872. It is also sometimes referred to as Huntington chorea, from a Greek word meaning "dance", referring to the characteristic movement disorder that is a part of the illness.

In 1976, the U.S. Congress mandated a Commission for the Control of Huntington's Disease and its consequences, and in 1979, Wexler became involved in a 20-year study that took her and team members to Venezuela. Fieldwork began in 1981. The researchers developed a pedigree of more than 18,000 individuals and collected more than 4,000 blood samples, which helped lead to the identification of the Huntington's disease gene at the tip of human chromosome 4. These same blood samples assisted in the mapping of other disease genes, including those responsible for familial Alzheimer's disease, kidney cancer, two kinds of neurofibromatosis, Amyotrophic Lateral Sclerosis (ALS), and dwarfism.

Wexler participated in the successful effort to create a chromosomal test to identify sufferers. She and other researchers developed a pre-symptomatic test that could tell who is carrying the fatal gene prior to the onset of symptoms. The samples the team collected were the key data allowing a global collaborative research group to locate the gene that causes the disease.

Bibliography

About Nancy Wexler, MA, MFCC, "http://www.nancy-wexler.com/bio.htm," July 23, 1997.

Bluestone, Mimi, "Science and Ethics: The Double Life of Nancy Wexler, " *Ms.*, November/December 1991, pp. 90-91.

Grady, Denise, "The Ticking of a Time Bomb in the Genes." *Discover*, June 1987.

Jaroff, Leon, "Making the Best of a Bad Gene," *Time*, February 10, 1992, pp. 78-79.

In 1974, Wexler earned a Ph.D. in clinical psychology from the University of Michigan, where she did her thesis on Huntington's disease, focusing on how it felt to be at risk for the disease.

Neither Wexler nor her sister has shown any symptoms of Huntington's disease, but both have contributed to the field of research. Alex Wexler, who has a Ph.D. in history, authored *Mapping Fate: A Memoir of Family, Risk, and Genetic Research*, which describes how the Wexlers coped with a diseased mother.

Hereditary Disease Foundation

Both daughters followed Milton Wexler's example and became involved in the foundation he started. Each soon became trustees of the Hereditary Disease Foundation.

Nancy Wexler is now president of the foundation, which raises funds for research on Huntington's and related inherited diseases, a goal that Wexler says will help create cure for the thousands of hereditary diseases that exist. The nonprofit foundation also sponsors interdisciplinary workshops for scientists who work on Huntington's and other genetic diseases

To demonstrate to scientists how the Huntington's gene looks in action, the foundation invites patients to interact with researchers at the beginning of each workshop. Wexler has said it is important for participants to observe what the gene can do its victims.

Bibliography

By Wexler

Applebaum, E and S. Firestein, eds. "A Case for Genetic Counseling: Review of A Genetic Counseling Casebook," *Contemporary Psychology*, 1985.

"Cracking the Code for Genetic Services: Issues in Policy Planning." (Presented at the Fifth Annual Research Conference on Bio-Psychological Dynamics in the Black Community at Howard University, June, 1977.)

"The Counselor and Genetic Disease: Huntington's Disease as a Model." ERIC Reports, *National Institute of Education*, DHEW, 1975.

"Foundation active in fight to cure Huntington's," *Nature*. 2007 July 19; 448 (7151): 250. (with C. Johnson).

Jeste, D. and R. Wyatt, eds. *"Huntington's Disease," Neuropsychiatry Movement Disorders*. Washington D.C.: American Psychiatric Press, Inc., 1984.

Emory, A. and Pullen, eds."Huntington's Disease and Other Late Onset Disorders," in *Psychological Aspects of Genetic Counseling*, 125-146. New York: Academic Press, 1984.

"Huntington's Disease in Venezuela: 7 Years of Follow-up on Symptomatic and Asymptomatic Individuals," *Movement Disorders*, 5:2:93-99, 1990.

"Venezuelan kindreds reveal that genetic and environmental factors modulate Huntington's disease age of onset," *Proceedings of the National Academy of Sciences*, 101(15): 3498-3503, 2004 (with Judith Lorimer et al.)

About Wexler

"An Interview with Dr. Nancy Wexler." *International Huntington Alliance*, 2012-07-30.

Wexler, Alex. *Mapping Fate: A Memoir of Family, Risk, and Genetic Research*. Berkeley, Calif.: University of California Press, 1995.

(Tsitsi D. Wakhisi)

Maurice H. F. Wilkins

Disciplines: Biology, genetics, and physics

Contribution: Wilkins' studies of the X-ray diffraction pattern of deoxyribonucleic acid (DNA) helped establish the double helix structure of the molecule.

Dec. 15, 1916	Born in Pongaroa, New Zealand
1922	Moves to England, where he enters the King Edward VI School
1938	Earns a degree in physics from the University of Cambridge
1938-1939	Conducts graduate research on radar at the University of Birmingham
1940	Earns a Ph.D. from St. John's College in Birmingham
1944	Relocates to the University of California, Berkeley
1945	Becomes a lecturer at the University of St. Andrews, Scotland
1946	Joins the faculty of King's College, London
1955-1970	Named deputy director of the biophysics unit of the Medical Research Council
1962-1970	Serves as a professor of molecular biology at King's College
1970-1972	Promoted to director of the biophysics unit, King's College
1970-1981	Named a professor of biophysics at King's College
1974-1980	Serves as director of biophysics unit of the Medical Research Council
1981	Named professor emeritus

Early Life

Maurice Hugh Frederick Wilkins was born on December 15, 1916, in Pongaroa, New Zealand, as the son of Irish immigrants. At the age of six, Wilkins was brought to England, where he attended the King Edward VI School in Birmingham.

In 1938, Wilkins graduated from the University of Cambridge with a degree in physics. He joined the Ministry of Home Security and Aircraft Production and, while at the same time working on his doctorate, conducted research in the newly developing technology of radar. In 1940, he was awarded his Ph.D. from St. John's College.

Great Britain was at war, and Wilkins carried on with his research in the Ministry of Home Security. He was assigned to the group working on the separation of uranium isotopes, a process later used in the development of the atomic bomb. In 1944, Wilkins relocated to the University of California, Berkeley, where he continued his work on isotope separation.

X-Ray Diffraction Studies of DNA

Although James D. Watson and Francis Crick are correctly noted for their achievement in determining the structure of deoxyribonucleic acid (DNA), the diffraction studies of Wilkins and Rosalind E. Franklin were critical in confirming that work.

In 1944, Oswald Avery and his coworkers demonstrated the role of DNA as genetic material in cells. The precise structure of the molecule, however, remained uncertain into the 1950s.

During World War II, Wilkins served as part of the British team assigned to the Manhattan Project, the U.S. development of the atomic bomb. Disillusioned by the ramifications of this work, Wilkins decided to apply his knowledge of physics to biology. In particular, he became interested in the structure of DNA and in 1946 began this research as a member of the faculty at King's College in London.

Although DNA was relatively easy to isolate, what appeared to be a complicated structure made it difficult to study. Initially, Wilkins observed a sample of DNA using a microscope, illuminating the molecule and observing the reflection of light. While manipulating the sample in a small volume of gelatin, he observed the fibrous nature of the DNA molecule.

Correctly assuming that if indeed DNA was a fiber, it should be amenable to X-ray diffraction studies, Wilkins began to analyze the material. In this procedure, X-rays were directed through a prepared crystalline sample of the material. Depending on the spacing of individual atoms in the DNA, the X-rays would be bent, or diffracted, into a pattern. Through analysis of the pattern, Wilkins hoped to work out a structure.

In 1951, Wilkins was joined at King's College by Franklin, a physical chemist who was prepared to carry out the research Wilkins had begun. Their professional relationship, while often less than smooth, would significantly complement each other's work.

The sharp pattern of the diffraction observed in the crystallography studies suggested certain characteristics for the DNA. The molecule was in the form of a spiral, or helix. Furthermore, the nucleotide bases that made up the DNA were observed in a regular pattern, suggesting a form of steps. Wilkins thought that the molecule was a double helix; because of its width, it was probably composed of two strands.

Watson and Crick correctly deduced the structure first. The diffraction studies carried out by both Wilkins and Franklin, however, quickly confirmed that Watson and Crick were correct in their suggestion of a double helix.

The teams of Watson and Crick and of Wilkins and Franklin published their work in the same issue of the journal *Nature* in 1953. Determination of the structure of the genetic material made possible the burgeoning field of molecular biology and later of biotechnology. Wilkins, Watson, and Crick were awarded the 1962 Nobel Prize in Physiology or Medicine for their work; Franklin had died in 1958.

Bibliography

Watson, James D. *The Double Helix*. New York: Signet Books, 1968.

Judson, Horace. *The Eighth Day of Creation*. Cold Spring Harbor, N.Y.: Cold Spring Harbor Press, 1996.

Olby, Robert. *The Path to the Double Helix*. Seattle, Wash.: University of Washington Press, 1974.

Research into DNA Structure

Like many physicists, after World War II, Wilkins became disheartened with the military applications of his research, and he began looking into other areas. Ultimately, his interest in biology was influenced by a book written by Erwin Schrödinger entitled *What Is Life?* (1944). In the book, Schrödinger suggests that physics could be applied to an understanding of life itself. In essence, he was creating a field called biophysics.

In 1945, Wilkins joined John Randall, his former professor, at the University of St. Andrews in Scotland. The next year, the two physicists became instrumental in the establishment of the Medical Research Council's biophysics unit at King's College in London, with the idea of merging the fields of physics and biology. Wilkins began his work on the structure of deoxyribonucleic acid (DNA).

By 1951, he had developed the X-ray diffraction techniques that he would use in deducing the structure of DNA. That year, he was also joined by Rosalind E. Franklin. Part colleagues and part competitors, Franklin and Wilkins spent most of the next two years trying to understand the pattern demonstrated by their DNA preparations.

They were beaten in this endeavor by James D. Watson and Francis Crick. Nevertheless, Wilkins and Franklin published their work in papers adjoining that of Watson and Crick.

Awards and Recognition

In 1962 Wilkins, Watson, and Crick were awarded the Nobel Prize in Physiology or Medicine. In 1959, Wilkins was named a Fellow of the Royal Society of King's College. He also received the Albert Lasker Award in 1960 and several honorary doctorates.

Wilkins continued his work with nucleic acids. In the 1960s, he began work on ribonucleic acid (RNA), showing that it too could possess a helical structure. He became director of the Medical Research Council's biophysics unit in 1970 and of its neurobiology unit in 1972. In 1981, he was named professor emeritus at King's College.

Bibliography

By Wilkins

"Physical Studies of Nucleic Acids: Nucleic Acid—An Extensible Molecule?," *Nature*, 1951 (with R. Gosling and W. Seeds).

"Molecular Structure of Deoxypentose Nucleic Acids," *Nature*, 1953 (with A. Stokes and H. Wilson).

"A New Configuration of Deoxyribonucleic Acid," *Nature*, 1958 (with D. Marvin and M. Spencer).

"Molecular Configuration of Nucleic Acids," *Science*, 1963.

"X-Ray Diffraction Study of the Structure of Nucleohistone and Nucleoprotamines," *Journal of Molecular Biology*, 1963 (with G. Zubay).

"A Note on Reversible Dissociation of Deoxyribonucleohistone," *Journal of Molecular Biology*, 1964 (with Zubay).

About Wilkins

Wasson, Tyler., ed. *Nobel Prize Winners: An H. W. Wilson Biographical Dictionary*. New York: H. W. Wilson, 1987.

Magill, Frank N., ed. *The Nobel Prize Winners: Physiology or Medicine*. Pasadena, Calif.: Salem Press, 1991.

McMurray, ed. Emily J. *Notable Twentieth-Century Scientists*. Detroit: Gale Research, 1995.

(Richard Adler)

Ian Wilmut

Areas of Achievement: Embryology and genetics

Contribution: Wilmut led the research group that first cloned a mammal—a lamb named Dolly—from an adult cell.

July 7, 1944	Born in Warwickshire, England
1967	Graduates from the University of Nottingham with a degree in agricultural science
1971	Receives Ph.D. at the University of Cambridge
1973	Creates the first calf ever produced from a frozen embryo, which he named Frosty
1974	Joins the Animal Breeding Research Station in Edinburgh, Scotland, (the Roslin Institute)
1988	Receives the Lord Lloyd of Kilgerran Award
1996	Produces a pair of lambs, Megan and Morag, from embryonic cells
1996	Successfully clones a sheep, Dolly, from a mammary cell of an adult sheep
1997	Announces Dolly's existence to the public
1999	Granted an Order for the British Empire (OBE)
2008	Knighted by Queen Elizabeth II for his services to science

Early Life

Born in Warwickshire, England, a year before the end of World War II, Wilmut grew up in the ancient town of Coventry, a place the Germans shelled heavily during the war. The family later moved north to Shipley, where Wilmut graduated from Scarborough Boys High School. His mother and his father, who had excelled in mathematics at the University of Cambridge, were school teachers. Wilmut's younger sister, Mary, became a teacher for children with special needs. Clearly the tradition of teaching was strong in the family, but Ian liked the outdoors, and had other ideas.

Ian Wilmut, who would shock the world with animal cloning, never might have made the achievement had he pursued either of his two childhood dreams. He first thought he would go to sea, either in the Royal Navy or the merchant service, but his color-blindness prevented that pursuit. He also considered a career in agriculture, and, at age 14, began working weekends on farms.

Hello, Dolly

Dolly, the first cloned sheep, launched a medical revolution in which cloning is now used to make stem cells that promise effective treatments for many major illnesses.

After receiving his Ph.D. Wilmut took a position at the Animal Breeding Research Station, an animal research institute in Scotland. In 1973, he produced the first calf (Frosty) born from a frozen embryo that had been implanted into a surrogate mother. Wilmut's idea for the experiment was to harvest cows that provide the best meat and milk by implanting their embryos into other females. With the ability to transfer embryos, cattle breeders could increase the quality of their animal stock.

Wilmut had heard that Danish embryologist, Dr. Steen M. Willadsen of Grenada Genetics in Texas, had used a cell from an embryo already in development to clone a sheep. Wilmut believed he could be successful in cloning an entire animal from a single adult cell.

The genetic data from four sheep were used in his and Keith Campbell's experiment in cloning. A cell was taken from a six-year-old sheep, the nucleus from which had been transplanted into an egg cell from a second sheep and then inserted into the uterus of a third sheep, and then a fourth, to develop. The creation of new sheep had entailed surgery on an egg much smaller than the tip of a sewing needle.

To achieve success, a total of 430 eggs were surgically removed from ewes. Each egg was stripped of its DNA and fused with an egg cell from a male ewe from which its genetic material had been removed. The egg and the cell were then fused with an electric current. Wilmut repeated the process successfully 277 times. Twenty-nine began to grow and divide into embryos.

Wilmut transferred the 29 embryos into surrogate mother sheep. Thirteen became pregnant. Only one of these 29 developed successfully inside a surrogate mother. Five months later on July 5, 1996, a healthy lamb named Dolly was born in a shed on the Roslin Institute farm. She weighed 14 pounds, 3 ounces. After seven months of monitoring Dolly's development, Wilmut told the world about Dolly (who was named after country-music entertainer, Dolly Parton).

In late November 1997, Dolly was successfully mated with a ram and her lamb was born on the morning of April 13, 1998. The birth of the lamb confirmed that while Dolly's embryonic origins were unique, she was able to breed normally and produce a healthy offspring.

Bibliography

"Autobiography of Ian Wilmut," The Shaw Prize, Sept. 9, 2008, http://www.shawprize.org/en/shaw.php?tmp=3&twoid=49&threeid=56&fourid=72&fiveid=14

"Ian Wilmut." in *Notable Scientists: From 1900 to the Present.* Detroit, Mich: Gale Group, 2008.

He later discovered he did not like the business end of commercial farming.

Wilmut studied agriculture at the University of Nottingham, where he embarked on scientific research for the first time. After a summer internship at a science laboratory, he turned his focus to animal science and graduated in 1967. With a concentration in animal genetic engineering, he received his doctorate at the University of Cambridge in 1971. His thesis was on the freezing of boar semen.

The Issue of Ethics

When news of Wilmut's cloned sheep Dolly was broadcast to the world, suspicions arose that if man could clone a sheep, it would be only a matter time before man would clone human beings. In published articles and before a March 1997, U.S. Senate public health and safety subcommittee hearing, Wilmut said his scientific research was not for the purpose of cloning humans but for the potential scientific benefits that could be gained from his research—treatments, for example, that could be used for diseased or damaged tissues or organs in humans.

Bibliography

By Wilmut

"Produce mammoth stem cells, says creator of Dolly the sheep," *The Conversation*, July 31, 2013, http://theconversation.com/produce-mammoth-stem-cells-says-creator-of-dolly-the-sheep-16335

The Second Creation: The Age of Biological Control by the Scientists Who Cloned Dolly. Headline Book Publishing, January 2000 (with Keith Campbell and Colin Tudge).

"After Dolly: The Promises and Perils of Cloning." W. W. Norton & Co., 2007 (with Roger Highfield).

About Wilmut

Highfield, Roger "Dolly creator Prof Ian Wilmut shuns cloning," *The Telegraph*, Nov. 16, 2007, http://www.telegraph.co.uk/science/science-news/3314696/Dolly-creator-Prof-Ian-Wilmut-shuns-cloning.html

"Dolly the Sheep Pioneer Knighted." BBC News. 29 December 2007, BBC News Online. http://news.bbc.co.uk/2/hi/health/7163108.stm (Accessed February 19, 2010).

"Ian Wilmut to Head Centre for Regenerative Medicine." University of Edinburgh, December 2, 2005. http://websiterepository.ed.ac.uk/news/051202stem.html (Accessed February 20, 2010).

"Ian Wilmut." World of Genetics. Gale, 2006. Biography In Context. Web. 2 Sept. 2013.

(Tsitsi D Wakhisi)

Glossary

Amino acid: Any organic molecule containing both at least one amine and one carboxyl (COOH) group. Amino acids are bound to form proteins.

Antigen: A molecule capable of stimulating the production of antibodies by an organism.

Bacteria (*sing.* bacterium): Single-celled organisms in which chromosomes are not carried in a nucleus. They may act as parasites and cause illness.

Bond: Any of several forces by which atoms or ions are held in a molecule or crystal. Most commonly, chemical bonds involve the sharing of one or more electrons between two atoms.

Cancer: One of a class of diseases characterized by abnormal cell growth that invades adjacent cell groups.

Catalyst: A substance that speeds up or makes possible a chemical reaction without being permanently changed itself. Enzymes are biological catalysts.

Chromosome: The threadlike structures, composed primarily of DNA, which contain most of the genetic information of a cell.

Crossing-over: The separation of linked genetic markers from their original chromosome and their recombination with another chromosome. This process usually involves a reciprocal exchange between two chromosomes.

DNA (deoxyribonucleic acid): The self-replicating molecule which is the fundamental carrier of hereditary material. Its structure is a double helix, a twisted ladder with sugars and phosphates forming the sides and base pairs in the center forming the rungs.

Dominant: Of a gene, requiring only one copy in order to be expressed as a given trait. *Compare* **Recessive**.

Enzyme: A protein with chemical groups on its surface that allow it to be a catalyst for a chemical reaction.

Frequency: For periodic motions, the number of complete cycles occurring per unit of time.

Gene: A portion of a DNA molecule that controls a hereditary characteristic of an organism, either individually or in combination with other genes.

Genome: All the genes contained in a single complete set of chromosomes.

Genotype: The genetic constitution of an individual with respect to one or more traits, even if those traits are not expressed. *Compare* **Phenotype**.

Grafting: The transplantation of some part of the body (especially skin) to another part of the body or to another patient.

Heredity: The transmission of characteristics from ancestor to descendant through genes.

Host: An organism that harbors and provides nourishment to parasites or microorganisms such as bacteria or viruses.

Immune system: An organism's system for responding to foreign materials and microorganisms through the production of antibodies.

Metabolism: The sum total of chemical reactions that occur in an organism, or a subset of those reactions pertaining to a defined function.

Mold: Any of various wooly fungal growths.

Molecule: A stable group of atoms held together by chemical forces and entering into characteristic chemical reactions.

Natural selection: The evolutionary process by which those organisms whose natural variations make them well suited to survival in the struggle to mature and reproduce are able to increase their frequency in the population. Over time, organisms in which many favorable variations accumulate diverge increasingly from their ancestors, creating new species.

Nucleic acid: Any of various acids, such as DNA and RNA, which are composed of chains of nucleotides.

Nucleotide: The structural unit of a nucleic acid, consisting of a sugar, a base, and a phosphate group.

Nucleus: The dense central portion of a cell containing chromosomes.

Parthenogenesis: A type of sexual reproduction in which an egg develops without the introduction of a sperm.

Phenotype: The observed characteristics of an organism, as they have developed as a result of the interaction between genetic and environmental factors. *Compare* **Genotype**.

Polymer: A long chain of identical chemical units that are linked to form a single large molecule.

Progeny: The offspring or descendants of an organism.

Radiation: The process of emitting energy in any form. Also, electromagnetic energy in the form of waves with a characteristic frequency, amplitude, and phase.

Reagent: One of the substances involved in a chemical reaction.

Recessive: Of a gene, requiring two copies in order to be expressed as a given trait. *Compare* **Dominant.**

Recombination: The formation of new combinations of genes in offspring that were not present in the parents. Recombination occurs either through the natural process of crossing-over or through artificial means, as in recombinant DNA technology.

RNA (ribonucleic acid): One of a class of nucleic acids containing the sugar ribose which are involved in the transcription and translation of the genetic material in DNA.

Transfusion: The direct injection of whole blood, plasma, or another solution into the bloodstream.

Transplantation: The removal of an organism or part of an organism from one environment and its introduction into another; often used to describe the removal of an organ or tissue from a donor to replace the defective organ or tissue of a recipient.

Variation: A group or character trait which is not true to a predetermined type.

Vector: An agent that carries an entity to a place where it can act; for example, ticks are vectors for the bacteria that produce Lyme disease in humans.

Virus: Any of a class of ultramicroscopic organisms containing nucleic acid and at least one protein. Viruses, which can reproduce only in living cells, often cause disease.

X chromosome: The sex chromosome which is always contributed by the female parent and which can be contributed by the male parent. Sex chromosomes determine an offspring's gender; humans normally have two, either XX (female) or XY (male). *Compare* **Y chromosome**.

Y chromosome: One of the two sex chromosomes which can be contributed only by the male parent. Sex chromosomes determine an offspring's gender; humans normally have two, either XX (female) or XY (male). *Compare* **X chromosome**.